Healing the Emptiness

A guide to emotional
and spiritual well-being

YASMIN MOGAHED

Published by IDIFY Publishing
www.idifyconsulting.com

Cover & Book Design: Gould Studio
www.gouldstudio.com

Interior Layout: Megan McCullough

ISBN: 979-8-9852918-1-0   Paperback
ISBN: 979-8-9852918-2-7   Digital

First Printing April 2022
Printed in Turkey by Elma Basim
Impress Digital

www.yasminmogahedtv.com
www.facebook.com/ymogahed
www.instagram.com/yasminmogahed
www.youtube.com/yasminmogahedonline
www.twitter.com/yasminmogahed

Dedication

I want to begin by expressing my deepest gratitude to God for giving me the ability to complete this book after years of turbulence in my life that made it difficult for me to write another book after *Reclaim Your Heart*. Truly the opening and the capacity to finally complete this heavy task came only from God. But I could not have done it without the people God blessed me with. First, I am deeply grateful to my husband and family for their unwavering support throughout this difficult journey. I could not have reached this point without them. I am also so thankful to my publisher, Chris Cornell, who has consistently shown the highest level of integrity, and proven to be one of the most reliable, consistent, and hard working people I've ever known. I am grateful to all my teachers who have helped shape me into who I am. And I am thankful to my talented designers, Peter Gould and his team, and to Zayd ul Islam and his Arabic team.

I have put my heart and soul into this book and I pray that it becomes a means of healing hearts for years to come.

Contents

Emptiness: The Origin

STEP ONE:
Diagnosing the Suffering

STEP TWO:
Removing Barriers to Healing

STEP THREE:

Treating the Wound

STEP FOUR:
Guarding the Heart

Redefining the Pain

Foreword

This is personal.

Several years ago I had a bad chemical burn on my face–especially concentrated on one half of my face. I got the burns from a bad reaction to a skin product I used and left on too long. Of course, life went on, so I needed to continue teaching. During one of my lectures, I remember it was in Ramadan. As is often the case when speaking at a Ramadan event or fundraiser, I stood on the podium between the people and their iftar. But just as the sun was setting, something I will always remember happened. The sun rays shone in through the window and hit just one half of my face. The scarred half. In that moment, it gave me peace, as I felt it was a message to me that this too will pass. And that my burns would heal.

My scars did heal and that difficult time in my life did pass, Alhamdulillah.

And every once in a while, it happens again.

A sun ray will hit my face. And in that moment I am reminded that whatever difficulty I am facing in that moment will also pass. Because no matter how dark the night gets, the sun always, always, rises again.

Emptiness: The Origin

At the Beginning

We all began with God. He created our heart and soul to know Him and love Him. When we were with God, we were whole. But then, the separation came. We had a noble journey to take. We were chosen to come down to this world. It was not a punishment. It was an honor given to mankind. We were chosen to represent God on this earth. God announced to the angels that He would create a representative on this earth: *Khalifah fil ard*. And what greater honor could there be than to be a deputy of God, a carrier of God's light and love in this world?

Here on earth, God would be unseen—but only to our eyes. We would see Him with our hearts. We would have to know Him through our souls. But unlike our original home, this world would not be perfect. There would be darkness. There would be cold. There would be long, dark nights sometimes. There would be storms, and there would be pain. Here, we would bleed. Here, we would experience the entirety of what it means to be human: vulnerable, frail, and in complete and desperate need for God. And then, this vulnerability would become our rope—our reminder of our Origin, and our Savior.

And saved we would be.

Just as we were sent on this worldly journey with the capacity to fall, we were also given the capacity to rise. Just as we would bleed, we would also heal. We would be designed with the divine capacity to cope. To survive. To even thrive through the storms. Each and every one of us would be given the God-given potential to see through the darkness. To rise through the cold. To break again and again, and to heal again and again. And then to be even more beautiful at the broken parts.

Allah would place within every single one of us everything we need to navigate all elements of this life: the good and the soul-crushing. When we came down to this earth, that same heart that was created for God, would become the compass by which we would find Him again. He would send us the Light of guidance to lead our hearts and to find Him in the midst of the fog and confusion of this life. Since the beginning of time, Allah has sent His messengers to bring us out of the pain of this world's darkness, into the Light of guidance.

The Quran says:

"(God) said, 'Descend from it (Paradise), all together, some of you as enemies of some others. But whenever guidance comes to you from Me, whoever follows My guidance will neither go astray nor suffer.'" (Quran 20:123)

قَالَ اهْبِطَا مِنْهَا جَمِيعًا بَعْضُكُمْ لِبَعْضٍ عَدُوٌّ فَإِمَّا يَأْتِيَنَّكُم مِّنِّي هُدًى فَمَنِ اتَّبَعَ هُدَايَ فَلَا يَضِلُّ وَلَا يَشْقَى ﴿١٢٣﴾

But throughout this journey, we still carry the original gash; this is the wound of Divine separation. Even beneath our own consciousness, we have an undeniable need to have our deepest wound healed by God. It is the very essence of our humanness, and our need. Our need for love. Our need for connection. Our need for security. Our need for acceptance. Our need for appreciation. Our need for understanding. Our need for significance. Our needs drive us in everything that we do. Until we meet Him. But beneath every single human need is a desperate call for our Origin. For our Healer and Redeemer.

For God.

And yet, since the beginning of time, mankind has tried to heal this prehistoric wound through everything–except God. We have sought to feel whole through our human relationships or our money or our status. We have sought to fill our vacancy by numbing it, through drugs, alcohol and physical satisfaction. We have spent our existence on this earth desperately trying to self-medicate. Searching everywhere for something to fill the emptiness.

But nothing else ever could.

Our soul was created by God, for God. We can never find true peace without knowing Him. We can never be whole without Him. He is the Healer. The wound inside us is a wound of Divine separation. How can it be healed through the material?

Many of us have lost our way in this life. Some people have given up hope, as they see no way out of their pain, their problems, their failures. Some people carry years of shame and self-hatred.

And some people are so sedated, they don't even know they're lost.

But there is hope. There is always hope. And there is a road back. The path of redemption, hope and mercy is always open to us, as long as our soul remains in our body. God wants every one of us to be healed and whole and in peace. But we cannot reject the Way if we want to arrive.

We must walk this path back Home, and we must walk it with our entire being.

In my own journey, I spent so many years struggling. When I was younger, I found countless reasons to be unhappy. And here is how: I *created* unhappiness by dwelling on every single thing I didn't like. This meant dwelling on the parts of my life that weren't perfect. It meant dwelling on the things that made me anxious or sad or disappointed. It meant focusing on the aspects of people around me that let me down, and dwelling on the moments that hurt me and then not letting go. It meant holding onto the past. But not the good stuff. Only the pain. It meant holding onto every time I felt let down or betrayed or hurt. I was very selective in my focus. I never thought about the things that were going well, because I had to focus my attention fully on "fixing" everything that wasn't. I didn't do this because I was trying to be negative. I did this for a very different reason. I did this for a reason that motivates many of us and also keeps many of us anxious and miserable: I was obsessed with "fixing things".

I was obsessed with the futile and misery-inducing project of making everything and every*one* "perfect". Without realizing it, I was literally *creating* my own unhappiness. I was holding onto my own daggers. And refusing to let them go. This human habit of ignoring the good things in our life, and focusing instead on all the things that make us anxious or scared or sad, seems to be "protective". In our mind, we presume that by fixating on what has gone wrong in the past and imagining all that *could* go wrong in the future, we will protect ourselves from more suffering. What we don't realize is that we end up creating the very suffering we are trying to avoid.

The Difference Between Pain and Suffering

There is a vast difference between *pain* and *suffering*. And this distinction is critical. Some level of pain is inevitable in this life. But, *suffering* is avoidable. Pain is designed to protect us from deeper harm. *Suffering is what happens when we ignore the warning sent by our pain.*

The challenge today is that we live in a world that does *not* understand this difference. And we are paying the price. Our modern culture operates as though pain should never exist. Our culture operates as if pain is an "oversight" of God. A great deal of this false belief comes from the idea that this life is all we have. In a "YOLO" (you only live once) culture, there will be a demand for this life to be perfect and pain-free. If we did indeed have only one life to live, of course we would demand that life to be perfect. So often we end up chasing illusions of happiness. We believe that if we could only gain the love, approval, power, money, and beauty that we seek, we could fill our emptiness.

Filling Our Emptiness

We live in a world where the moment we feel pain, we find ourselves surrounded by countless sedatives, promising to take it away. Sex, drugs, alcohol, materialism, consumerism are some of the many escapes we use to distract ourselves from what hurts in our lives. And some of us use other sedatives. Some of us try to lose ourselves in our work and our careers. Some people try to fill the void by "living online". We disengage from our real life and our *real relationships* in order to hide in a false social media world, or in our devices and technology. We become dependent upon the immediate and temporary dopamine rush of social approval. We begin to covet likes and followers and share intimate aspects of our lives in the public sphere, waiting for commentary and praise. Waiting to be seen–even if it's by perfect strangers.

And yet all along, we only become more empty and even more isolated.

One study published in the *American Journal of Preventive Medicine* found that the group who spent the most hours per day on social media had 3 times the risk of developing depression. Another study published in the *Journal of Social and Clinical Psychology* randomly assigned one group to reduce their social media usage to only 30 mins (10 mins Facebook, 10 mins Instagram, 10 mins Snapchat). The study found that reducing social media usage decreased depression, anxiety and loneliness. Jordyn Young, a co-author of the paper from the University of Pennsylvania wrote: "What we found overall is that if you use less social media, you are actually less depressed and less lonely–meaning that the decreased social media use is what causes that qualitative shift in your well-being." This was the first study to establish a causal link between social media usage and depression, anxiety, and loneliness.

Purpose of Pain

Our attempts to hide from our pain through social media end up doing the opposite. And what this pain avoidance culture fails to recognize is that even pain itself serves a purpose. Pain is a messenger. It is often a protective measure. It points us towards what needs to change in our lives, in ourselves, and in our relationships. It tells us which habits we need to abandon. And which habits we desperately need to adopt. Often, pain demands that we address hidden wounds that need healing.

As Geoff MacDonald, professor of psychology at the University of Toronto, put it: "Pain is really good at disrupting attention and getting you singularly focused on making the bad thing stop." A fascinating review of more than 500 neuroscience studies found that the pain of heartbreak activated the same areas of the brain as physical pain. But just like physical pain, we often try to ignore and numb the pain of heartbreak.

Years ago, I read an article that really stuck with me. It was about a man who went to the dentist with severe tooth pain. The doctor told him that he had an infection which was causing his excruciating pain. The dentist prescribed two types of medication for the patient. One medication was a painkiller to help him manage the throbbing. The other prescription was an antibiotic to treat the infection itself. However, this man could not afford both drugs, so he opted for the one most of us choose. He chose the pain killer. He successfully numbed his pain. But soon the infection grew and spread to his brain. The man died.

What began as a simple, treatable infection, ended up killing him. How did this happen? And why? The pain he was feeling in his tooth was actually designed to protect him. It was screaming to him that something was wrong inside him and it needed to be treated immediately. The purpose of the pain was to sound an alarm inside of him, so he would address the problem, and fix it at the root. Instead, he sought to just make the pain go away, without addressing the root cause of that pain. And as a result, it killed him.

And this is exactly what many of us do with our emotional pain. We don't address the root cause. Instead, we just try to numb it. For the man with the tooth pain, his actual problem was *not* the pain. His problem was the infection. The pain was only a symptom. *So the man was treating the wrong ailment.*

M. Scott Peck, author of *The Road Less Traveled,* writes: "Rather than being the illness, the symptoms are the beginning of its cure. The fact that they are unwanted makes them all the more a phenomenon of grace–a gift of God, a message from the unconscious, if you will, to initiate self-examination and repair."

Our pain is like a smoke alarm. We want it to stop, but it serves a purpose. When the smoke alarm goes off, we could simply just take out the batteries. This will give us momentary peace from the noise. But the purpose of the alarm is to let us know that there's a fire in our home. The fire starts out small, but if we ignore the alarm–and ignore the actual problem–what began as only a spark, can burn our entire house down.

Many of us suffer for this exact reason. **When we feel emotional or psychological pain, we often seek a *sedative*, rather than a *cure*.** Often, we just want to 'take the batteries out' of our pain. Just make it quiet. Make it go away. We look to numb the hurt, rather than search deeper, beyond the surface, to find the root cause of it. To find the root cause of the alarm. And then address it.

This inner search requires courage and honesty. And it's hard. It's uncomfortable. So many of us avoid it at any cost. We opt for what's easier; but ironically, this is what leads to our own suffering. *Suffering is what happens when we repeatedly ignore the message of our pain.* Suffering is what happened to the man, only after he ignored the tooth pain, and did not address the underlying cause (an infection). It's what happens when we muffle the alarm, but allow our home to burn down.

Sometimes when we feel empty, we don't realize that our soul is crying out. That our heart is starving for God. Instead, we look to distract ourselves with other things, other people, other activities.

Emotional and psychological pain are as inevitable as physical pain in this life. No matter how much we may love our child, no matter how much we may try to protect them, it is impossible for our child to never fall. To never feel pain, to never cut, scrape, or even break parts of their body. It is an inevitable part of dunya (worldly life). Similarly, some sadness, fear, loss, grief, and worry is inevitable in this life. Allah says:

"And We will surely test you with something of fear and hunger and a loss of wealth and lives and fruits, but give good tidings to those who patiently persevere." (Quran 2:155)

وَلَنَبْلُوَنَّكُمْ بِشَيْءٍ مِنَ الْخَوْفِ وَالْجُوعِ وَنَقْصٍ مِنَ الْأَمْوَالِ وَالْأَنْفُسِ وَالثَّمَرَاتِ وَبَشِّرِ الصَّابِرِينَ ﴿١٥٥﴾

Emotions Serve a Purpose

In fact, some negative emotion is not only inevitable–it is necessary. If a person never experienced *any* sadness or fear or anger about *anything*, that would be a sign of mental illness or unhealed trauma. To experience absolutely no sadness, anger, or fear would be unhealthy. Trials at some level are a necessary part of our human experience. When we react in a healthy way, trials make our hearts softer and more humble. Trials can deepen our sense of empathy and compassion and reliance on God. Everything which God does serves a purpose. This includes emotion. Our feelings–both positive and negative–were created for a purpose. They motivate us to grow and rectify ourselves and the world around us. Imagine what would happen if injustice did *not* make us angry. Would we fight to change it? Imagine if danger of potential harm did not make us afraid? Would we take action to protect ourselves and those around us from that harm? Would we run to Allah for help and protection? Would we sincerely turn to Him in humility and need if we never felt fear?

If heart disease did not cause chest pain, would we turn to the doctor for surgery?

We do not suffer because of negative emotions. We suffer when those emotions are not *regulated*, or they begin to consume or paralyze us. Emotion is normal and healthy when it is regulated by our *"Aql"* (mind). The word *"Aql"* in Arabic literally means "the tying of something". The function of our mind (Aql) is to "tie" or manage/regulate our emotions and desires. Emotions are the driving force–like the acceleration in a car. And the *Aql* is like the brakes. We need the acceleration to function in order to move anywhere. If the acceleration breaks down (if the person has no emotion), the car will stand still. But we also need working brakes. If we have a car with *only* acceleration, but no working brakes (emotional regulation/Aql), we will crash.

Resilience

In one of my favorite quotes, Albert Camus writes, "In the midst of hate, I found there was, within me, an invincible love. In the midst of tears, I found there was, within me, an invincible smile. In the midst of chaos, I found there was, within me, an invincible calm. I realized, through it all, that…In the midst of winter, I found there was, within me, an invincible summer. And that makes me happy. For it says that no matter how hard the world pushes against me, within me, there's something stronger–something better, pushing right back."

We have lived through unprecedented times. Trials have always faced nations throughout time. But, for the first time in recent history, we have faced a trial that was not just isolated to one location or community. The Coronavirus pandemic hit globally. The whole world locked down. Death did not discriminate. The rich and the poor, the powerful, and the weak, were all touched by this trial.

Although there were discrepancies in resources, and access to medical treatment, etc., it was a shared experiential challenge throughout the world. There was a widespread level of chronic stress. There was ongoing fear and an ongoing sense of uncertainty. And as human beings, we struggle deeply with uncertainty because it makes many people feel powerless. When we don't know what's coming, that uncertainty often causes a great deal of anxiety and stress. During the lockdown, more people struggled with depression and other mental health challenges. Incidents of domestic violence increased. And so, the topic of resilience has become of utmost relevance.

The definition of resilience, according to the American Psychological Association is: "The process of adapting well in the face of adversity, trauma, tragedy, threats or significant sources of stress."

Human beings differ in their capacity to be resilient. A forest fire doesn't affect every tree the same. A Sequoia, for example, is almost fireproof. The question is, can our hearts be like the Sequoia? And even deeper, can we as human beings reach a level even higher than just survival? When you examine the definition of resilience, you find that it refers to coping and *surviving* in the face of challenges. But what if there was something even greater? What if human beings could do even more than just *survive* in their storms?

What if we could *thrive* in our storms? What if there was something even higher than resilience?

Take for example your phone. If you drop your cell phone and you have a very effective protective case, your cell phone will *survive* the drop. It *survives* that "stressful situation". It doesn't break. But does it grow? Does your cell phone become faster or more efficient through the fall? Does your cell phone gain anything by that fall itself? Naturally, it does not. So, we say your phone was *resilient* in that situation. It *survived*; but it did not *thrive*.

As human beings, we have the capacity to be better than the cell phone. We have the capacity to not only survive our stresses and challenges, but we also actually have the capacity to *grow* and *thrive* through our stresses and challenges. And that makes human beings extremely unique. In contrast to the cell phone, take for example the immune system. Ever wonder why Covid-19 caused minor to no symptoms in some people, while for others, it was deadly? How can the same stressor (the virus) affect two people so differently? What differentiates these two people? The answer all comes down to one thing: the strength of the immune system and its response. It comes down to the strength of the individual's ability to withstand and combat—and then ultimately overcome—the onslaught. The trial.

And then those who *do* overcome, do not only survive; they actually become stronger *because of* the trial. They develop an immunity to that virus. That's the entire concept of a vaccine. A vaccine is introducing a stressor to the body at a lesser level, a weaker level. But by introducing that stressor, we teach the body how to grow, how to strengthen itself so that it actually leaves that experience, that challenge, stronger than it was before. It doesn't come out the same. The same essential threat that killed others, has only built them stronger. This is profound. Our spiritual and psychological immune system is our ability to not only withstand and overcome, but even grow through our spiritual and psychological challenges.

The Stockdale Paradox

The Stockdale Paradox holds that you must retain faith that you will prevail in the end, regardless of the difficulties, while at the same time, you must confront the most brutal facts of your current reality, whatever they might be. The paradox was named after Admiral Jim Stockdale, who was the highest-ranking United States military officer in the "Hanoi Hilton" prisoner-of-war camp during the height of the Vietnam War. Stockdale was tortured more than 20 times during his eight years of imprisonment.

In his book, *Good to Great*, Jim Collins describes his conversation with Stockdale after his release. Collins asked Stockdale how he survived. Stockdale explains: "I never lost faith in the end of the story. I never doubted not only that I would get out, but also that I would prevail in the end and turn the experience into the defining event of my life, which, in retrospect, I would not trade."

Collins then asks, "Who didn't make it out?"

"Oh, that's easy," Stockdale said. "The ones who said, 'We're going to be out by Christmas.' And Christmas would come, and Christmas would go. Then they'd say, 'We're going to be out by Easter.' And Easter would come, and Easter would go. And then Thanksgiving, and then it would be Christmas again. And they died of a broken heart…This is a very important lesson. You must never confuse faith that you will prevail in the end–which you can never afford to lose–with the discipline to confront the most brutal facts of your current reality, whatever they might be."

Stockdale describes how he admonished the others, saying: "We're not getting out by Christmas; deal with it!"

What Stockdale experienced is a powerful phenomenon. He never lost hope. But he was not in denial either. He did not hide from the reality of his current situation. He did not pretend or hold onto delusional positivity. Instead, he accepted the reality of his current situation, while at the same time never losing hope of things getting better. This, in psychology, is called the "Stockdale Paradox". In Islam, this is Sabr (patience), combined with hope. This is the believer in hardship.

If we examine just one example of the Prophets, we get a glimpse into this perfect balance. The duaa of Prophet Ayoub (AS) is an amazing example of this phenomenon. He was at his lowest point. He had lost his health, his wealth, and his family. At his hardest point, after 18 years of being tried, he turned to Allah and called out:

"And [mention] Job, when he called to his Lord, 'Indeed, adversity has touched me, and you are the Most Merciful of the merciful.'" (Quran 21:83)

وَأَيُّوبَ إِذْ نَادَى رَبَّهُ أَنِّى مَسَّنِيَ الضُّرُّ وَأَنْتَ أَرْحَمُ الرَّاحِمِينَ ۝

There are several profound lessons to learn from the duaa of Prophet Ayoub (AS). First, he is not hiding his pain from Allah. He is not numbing it and he is not pretending that it doesn't exist. He is not hiding from reality. He is turning to Allah *with* his pain and being honest and vulnerable. This is the first essential step towards healing: Acknowledging the wound itself, and then taking it to Allah to heal it. But what's especially powerful about his response is his hope in the midst of his greatest anguish: "...and you are the Most Merciful of the merciful."

This is the attitude of a believer in hardship. When they see the darkness surround them, they don't feign "false positivity" by pretending that it isn't dark in that moment. They acknowledge the darkness of the night, *while at the same time* having full hope and certainty that the sun will rise again. And their hope is *ultimately* in God: "...and you are the Most Merciful of the merciful."

It is also essential that the believer does not try to set the time frame. Sabr requires submission to God's time frame—not ours.

When a believer follows this process, Allah saves them. Every time:

"So We responded to him and removed what afflicted him of adversity. And We gave him [back] his family and the like thereof with them as mercy from Us and a reminder for the worshippers [of Allah]." (Quran 21:84)

فَاسْتَجَبْنَا لَهُ فَكَشَفْنَا مَا بِهِ مِنْ ضُرٍّ وَآتَيْنَاهُ أَهْلَهُ وَمِثْلَهُمْ مَعَهُمْ رَحْمَةً مِنْ عِنْدِنَا وَذِكْرَى لِلْعَابِدِينَ ۝

For the believer, the help of God always comes; but it is crucial to understand that it does not always come in the form we expect. Allah may not cure the sickness, but He could place tranquility in the heart of the sick. Allah may not change the situation externally, but instead change your heart.

This phenomenon is not about "fake positivity" or "spiritual bypassing". It is about the real help of Allah. And that comes *in this life*. It is Divine law. "Inna ma'al 'usri yusra": "Verily *with* the hardship, comes ease" (Quran 94:6). The ease may not be in reference to the particular hardship (the dead do not come back to life; the sick may not survive). But the ease and help of Allah will come in other aspects of your life and inside you. Allah held together the heart of Umm Musa, but she still had to part from her child. While Asiyah (AS) was to be tortured, she was shown her place in jannah, so she smiled just before leaving this world. Maryam (AS) was given dates as comfort from Allah in the midst of pain so great that she wished she had died and been forgotten. When the companions were suffering from war, death, torture, and starvation, Allah says:

"Remember when He covered you with drowsiness, as tranquility (descending) from Him and sent down water from the sky to cleanse you, to remove Satan's pollution from you, to make your hearts strong and your feet firm." (Quran 8:11)

In the Battle of Uhud, the Muslims experienced a similar experience as described above (Al'Imran 3:154). On both occasions, when their conditions should have produced intense fear and panic among them, God filled their hearts with such peace and tranquility that they were overpowered with drowsiness.

Sometimes the ease and help of Allah is in keeping your feet firm and giving you internal peace. For example, the People of the Ditch is a story mentioned in Surat Al Buruj about a group of believers who were placed in a ditch and killed by their tyrannical ruler. These believers were still killed, but the help and ease was that Allah kept their feet firm (istiqama) and they died with their faith strong. In fact, narrations tell us that one of the women was holding her newborn child and was about to retreat. Then Allah made her child speak and reassure her that she was on the Truth. For them, the help of Allah came in keeping their hearts firm, even in the face of tyranny. For a believer, God gives ease in this life and the next. Even when death does come to the believer, there is ease in the departing of the soul (surat al-Naziat) and in the grave, and Hereafter.

I have a close friend who had to watch 3 of her children die slowly in front of her eyes due to a rare genetic disorder called MPS. And while she was going through all that, she told me she was "drowning in gratitude". It's not a cliche, but Allah did something miraculous in her heart. And that is the ease. That is the miracle.

Several years ago, I reconnected with Dr. Jitmoud, my principal from a school I used to teach at. While speaking with him, I found out that his son had recently been murdered while delivering pizzas. What my principal said next absolutely shocked me. Dr. Jitmoud told me that he wanted to meet the murderer so that he could forgive him; he wanted to tell him about Islam, because he wanted the murderer "to be in the same place with his son in the hereafter."

These incidents are not fairytales. They are real. They are signs of what the help of God looks like in this life. And they are signs of the miracles that true faith and reliance can do inside the heart.

Beyond Just Resilience

As we examine how hardships affect us, we realize that not everyone comes out the same. One gust of wind can completely uproot some trees, while leaving other trees firm and growing.

Consider the powerful divine sign (ayah) of fire. A forest fire is actually necessary for the survival and growth of the forest itself. The fire itself supports the natural cycle of growth and replenishment by clearing dead trees, leaves and competing vegetation from the forest floor. These fires make room for stronger trees to grow by removing weak or diseased trees and breaking down and returning nutrients to the soil.

So, the problem isn't the fire. In fact, the fire itself is necessary for the survival of the forest.

The problem is when the fire gets out of control and begins to consume more than it should. What happens when the emotional and psychological fires of our life get out of control and consume more than they should? What happens when our emotional experience becomes imbalanced? How can we prevent normal pain from turning into suffering?

We will never be able to stop the storms from hitting our lives. We will never be able to hold back the waves. We will never control the weather. But Allah has given us shelter. He has given us the lifeboat. And He has given us a sort of *spiritual and emotional immune system*.

The Prophet (pbuh) taught us this principle: *"**Know Allah in ease and He will know you in hardship.** And know that what has passed you by, was never meant to befall you. And what has befallen you, was never meant to pass you by. And know that victory comes with patience, relief with affliction, and with hardship comes ease."* (Hadith Nawawi 19)

In another hadith, the Prophet (pbuh) says: "Whoever would be pleased for Allah to answer him during times of hardship and difficulty, let him supplicate often during times of ease." (Sahih, Tirmidhi 3382)

By being close to Allah during our times of ease, we are building our immune system. Every prayer, every ayah, every sajdah, every duaa, every act of service to others, every charity is another building block in that immune system–the very system that will later fight for us when a threat hits. When–not if–the test comes.

As we go through this life, there are the *ahkam al share'e* (decrees in Islamic law) and *ahkam al kawni* (decrees in the universe). Those who strive to have sabr in the decrees of divine law (sharia), God will give them sabr in the decrees of the universe. Ibn ul Qayyim (RA) wrote: "Those who strive to guard His outward commands of servitude (Ubudiyah), He gives them patience to bear His decrees of Lordship (Rububiyah)."

Allah says:

...and he who transgresses the bounds set by God does injustice to himself... (Quran 65:1)	وَمَنْ يَتَعَدَّ حُدُودَ اللَّهِ فَقَدْ ظَلَمَ نَفْسَهُ

When we break God's rules in our lives, we only hurt ourselves–not Allah. If a patient chooses to drink poison instead of his medicine, he doesn't hurt the doctor. He hurts only himself.

When Worship or Obedience is Hard

Yet, often we still find ourselves struggling to obey the commands of Allah. We may struggle with salah (prayer) or hijab or staying away from the haram (forbidden). It is important to understand that our faith (iman) is like a tree. And our actions are like the fruits. When the fruit of any tree is diseased, or the branches are unhealthy, we don't heal the fruit or the branches; we must heal the roots. We must look at the health of the soil. When we find ourselves unwilling to obey a Divine commandment, or when any act of worship becomes too difficult, we must look at the roots of our relationship with Allah. For example, when we find hijab too difficult, or salah too heavy, we must look at the master of the body–the heart.

Ayesha (RA) said: "(Be informed) that the first thing that was revealed thereof was a chapter from *Al-Mufassil*, and it mentioned Paradise and the Fire. After the people embraced Islam, the verses regarding legal and illegal things were revealed. If the first thing to be revealed was: 'Do not drink alcoholic drinks.' people would have said, 'We will never leave alcoholic drinks,' and if it had been revealed, 'Do not commit illegal sexual intercourse', they would have said, 'We will never give up illegal sexual intercourse.'" (Sahih al-Bukhari 4993)

Our Mother, Ayesha (RA) is explaining an essential concept. Once a person has *embraced* Islam wholeheartedly and submitted to God, obedience to the rules becomes easier. We must address the roots before healing the branches. If we find ourselves unable to obey the rules of God, we need to examine the roots and the soil. We must examine our bond of love, hope and healthy fear of God. When this is all healthy, the fruits, the actions, will be healthy.

Two things cause the roots of the tree of iman (faith) to be weak and unhealthy.

LACK OF NOURISHMENT

The first cause of depleted soil is lack of nourishment or *ghafla* (heedlessness). When our lives lack the water and oxygen of *thikr*, (remembrance: salah, athkar, Quran), the tree will suffer and cannot grow properly. We will see the result as unhealthy or rotten fruit (actions). The cure is the remembrance of Allah.

WEEDS OR TOXICITY IN THE SOIL

The second cause of unhealthy soil is weeds or toxicity. The fruits of our actions can never be healthy if our soil is poisoned by the weeds of sin and a toxic environment, friends, habits, or input from the eyes, ears and tongue. The cure for this poison is istighfar (repentance is removing the weeds), and a healthy environment, companionship, habits, and input through the eyes, ears and tongue (this is the food of the soil).

The Prophet (pbuh) told us about a man who killed 100 people.

حَدَّثَنَا مُحَمَّدُ بْنُ بَشَّارٍ حَدَّثَنَا مُحَمَّدُ بْنُ أَبِي عَدِيٍّ عَنْ

شُعْبَةَ عَنْ قَتَادَةَ عَنْ أَبِي الصِّدِّيقِ النَّاجِيِّ عَنْ أَبِي سَعِيدٍ

ـ رضى الله عنه ـ عَنِ النَّبِيِّ صلى الله عليه وسلم قَالَ

كَانَ فِي بَنِي إِسْرَائِيلَ رَجُلٌ قَتَلَ تِسْعَةً وَتِسْعِينَ إِنْسَانًا

ثُمَّ خَرَجَ يَسْأَلُ فَأَتَى رَاهِبًا فَسَأَلَهُ فَقَالَ لَهُ هَلْ مِنْ تَوْبَةٍ

قَالَ لاَ فَقَتَلَهُ فَجَعَلَ يَسْأَلُ فَقَالَ لَهُ رَجُلٌ ائْتِ قَرْيَةَ كَذَا

وَكَذَا فَأَدْرَكَهُ الْمَوْتُ فَنَاءَ بِصَدْرِهِ نَحْوَهَا فَاخْتَصَمَتْ فِيهِ

مَلاَئِكَةُ الرَّحْمَةِ وَمَلاَئِكَةُ الْعَذَابِ فَأَوْحَى اللَّهُ إِلَى هَذِهِ أَنْ

تَقَرَّبِي وَأَوْحَى اللَّهُ إِلَى هَذِهِ أَنْ تَبَاعَدِي وَقَالَ قِيسُوا مَا

بَيْنَهُمَا فَوُجِدَ إِلَى هَذِهِ أَقْرَبُ بِشِبْرٍ فَغُفِرَ لَهُ

The Prophet (pbuh) said, "Amongst the men of Bani Israel there was a man who had murdered ninety-nine persons. Then he set out asking (whether his repentance could be accepted or not). He came upon a monk and asked him if his repentance could be accepted. The monk replied in the negative and so the man killed him. He kept on asking till a man advised to go to such and such village. (So he left for it) but death overtook him on the way. While dying, he turned his chest towards that village (where he had hoped his repentance would be accepted), and so the angels of mercy and the angels of punishment quarreled amongst themselves regarding him. Allah ordered the village (towards which he was going) to come closer to him, and ordered the village (whence he had come), to go far away, and then He ordered the angels to measure the distances between his body and the two villages. So he was found to be one span closer to the village (he was going to). So he was forgiven." (Sahih al-Bukhari 3470)

There are many lessons that can be derived from this hadith. First, it provides hope to anyone who thinks they have sinned too much to be forgiven, or that they have strayed too far away to come back to God or religion. This man killed 100 people. And even for him there was redemption. Another important lesson in this hadith is the importance of environment. When this man wanted to redeem himself, he was advised to *change his environment*.

The Purpose of Trials

We are all tested in different ways. Some people are tested in their health, while others are tested in their wealth. When health is given to us, how do we use it? When wealth is given to us, how do we spend it? And then when health or wealth is taken from us, how do we respond? Our trials also serve many purposes in this life and the next. Our trials can cure us, purify us, strengthen us, and bring us back to who we were meant to be. They prepare us to meet our Creator with a beautiful heart. That heart will be covered with scars, but each one of those scars will mark how this life tried to defeat us, but never could.

Tests as Cure

Be careful. Many people believe that Allah tests us only to see what we will do. Yes. He sees our response. But keep in mind, He already knows how we will react in any given moment. He knows all that is in front or behind us. He is the Creator of time itself. So look deeper. Tests don't just show us to God. Tests show us to ourselves. If we have a disease that is hidden deep within our hearts, if we have a weakness hidden deep inside, tests will reveal them. Tests are not meant to humiliate us. Tests are meant to identify the disease or weakness, so we can be cured and strengthened.

When I was a teenager, my diabetic father started getting chest pain. He went several times to his doctor, who misdiagnosed his chest pains as "spasms of the trachea" and gave him an inhaler. For four years, my father never knew what was actually broken inside. Then one day, in the summer of 1998, my father did a "stress test" with a radioactive marker. That day, my dad found out that he had close to 100 percent blockage of many of his heart vessels. The doctors didn't let him leave the hospital and he had to undergo emergency quadruple bypass surgery.

When a heart patient comes to a doctor, he undergoes a "stress test". This means his body and especially his heart, are put through a "stressful" situation (running on a treadmill), in order to identify where the heart blockage is located. Once the problem is identified, it can be treated. And what do we say to a doctor who puts us through such a test? Do we consider the doctor "cruel"? Do we show anger? No. In fact, we *pay* the doctor to do so. And then we show only gratitude for subjecting us to a literal stress test because it saved our life.

Tribulation reveals what's inside. Observe yourself when you are tested. What you see is what's hidden inside. Why does Allah bring it out? It is out of mercy that Allah reveals what is hidden, first to ourselves. He reveals it so that it can be cured. Before a doctor can begin the process of treatment, the first step is proper diagnosis. Trials are like an X-Ray done on the spiritual heart. It will allow us to see the diseases that are hidden deep within ourselves. It reveals the cracks, so they can be repaired.

What can our trial tell us about ourselves and those around us? The Quran teaches us that we are given tests "so that Allah would reveal what is in your chests and purify that which is deep in your heart" (Quran 3:154). We must ask: what has this trial revealed about me? How strong was my spiritual immune system? That's exactly what Allah does through balaa' (hardships/tests). He reveals us. To ourselves, first. But He also reveals us to others.

Consider what the Coronavirus pandemic revealed. Some people were found deliberately trying to infect others, while others risked their lives and the lives of their families to save others. Some people used it as an opportunity to hoard or jack up prices. While others used the opportunity to give of their wealth and time for the sake of serving others.

As a result of this global crisis, most of the world went into lockdown. Research conducted by Austrian, British and Belgian scientists, found that during the peak of lockdown in April 2020, the number of people reporting depression and anxiety reached 52 percent–three times more than the pre-Covid-19 average of only 17 percent.

This global trial also revealed many of the "cracks" that we had internally, both individually and collectively. The National Domestic Violence Hotline reported a significant increase in domestic violence during the lockdown.

One could argue that the crisis *caused* these problems. *But perhaps the crisis doesn't **cause** our problems. Perhaps the crisis only **reveals** our problems.* Perhaps our trials bring what is hidden to the surface, so it can be addressed. And healed. Consider the phrase "coming to a head". What does it refer to? According to the Cambridge Dictionary, it means to "reach a point where some strong action has to be taken." The origin of the phrase dates back to the 1800's and refers to a "boil coming to a head and getting ready to burst. A boil is an infection that forms under the skin. A red lump starts to form and it slowly fills with white pus. After a few days the boil turns white and the pus is ready to come out."

Allah (swt) does not want us to remain in suffering. If there is an infection under the surface, deep within our hearts or in our lives, Allah wants us to take action to heal it. Trials serve as a massive microscope on our lives. The diseases threatening our well-being can no longer hide under the magnifying power of trials.

Through these trials, both individual and collective, Allah shines a spotlight on the weak link in our own immune system, and the collective immune system of the world. It is pure Divine mercy to reveal what's sick, so it can be healed. To show us what's broken, so that it can be fixed. And strengthened. Then the question is: how? How can we not only survive our difficulties, but thrive within our difficulties?

ANTI-FRAGILE AND JAPANESE ART

Ernest Hemingway wrote, "The world breaks everyone. And afterward, many are strong at the broken places."

Kintsugi is the Japanese art of repairing broken pottery with powdered gold, silver or platinum. This is due to the belief that something is *more* beautiful after it has been broken and repaired; and that our breaks should be part of our story—rather than something we hide. The human heart has the capacity to be like this Japanese art.

In his book, *Anti-Fragile: Things That Gain from Disorder*, Nassim Nicholas Taleb discusses a profound concept. He defines "anti-fragility" as the ability to actually benefit and improve because of disruptions, volatility and uncertainty. Human beings have this God-given capacity to not only survive—but thrive and grow through uncertainty and challenges.

POST TRAUMATIC GROWTH

The phenomenon of growing through challenges was termed: "Post Traumatic Growth". In the past, there was a lot of work on Post Traumatic Stress Disorder (PTSD). PTSD is "anxiety that develops in some people after extremely traumatic events, such as combat, crime, an accident or natural disaster." People with PTSD may relive the event via intrusive memories, flashbacks and nightmares; they may avoid anything that reminds them of the trauma and have anxiety that disrupts their life.

Many of these studies looked at *surviving* trauma. But new research on post traumatic growth found that some people come out of trauma with a *renewed* appreciation for life. The Post-traumatic Growth Inventory surveys how people respond to adversity to drive personal development, and it covers five dimensions: new possibilities, relating to others, personal strength, appreciation of life, and spiritual change.

Allah and His messenger (pbuh) talk about post traumatic growth throughout the Quran and sunnah.

Tests as Purification

There are times when tests are given to purify us. The Prophet (pbuh) said: "No calamity befalls a Muslim but that Allah expiates some of his sins because of it, even if it were the prick of a thorn." *(Volume 7, Book 70, Number 544)*

In another hadith, The Prophet said, "No fatigue, nor disease, nor sorrow, nor sadness, nor hurt, nor distress befalls a Muslim, even if it were the prick of a thorn, but that Allah expiates some of his sins for that." *(Volume 7, Book 70, Number 545)*

As one great poet wrote: "When someone beats a rug, the beating is not intended for the rug. It is intended for the dirt inside the rug." For example, the heating of gold is not meant to destroy the gold. It is meant to purify it. Like gold, Allah speaks in the Quran about the purification of the believers through trial. When gold is heated, impurities are removed. When the heart of the believer goes through trials, impurities are removed.

Allah says:

"And that Allah may purify the believers [through trials] and destroy the disbelievers." (Quran 3:141)

Tests to Strengthen & Benefits of Trials

When we study the creation, we can learn many truths about the sunnah (way) of Allah. For example, when we break a bone, and that bone heals, the bone actually becomes stronger at the place it broke. Our worldly trials can do the same thing. One of the great scholars of our tradition, Al-`Izz Ibn`Abdus-Salam, wrote his famous treatise about the 17 benefits of tribulation.

He discusses how trials lead us to realize Allah's power over us. It is easy to get lost in an illusion of control over our lives. We often believe that *we* are the drivers of our lives. We think *we* are in control. We carry this soul crushing pressure to keep everything in place and fix everything that's broken. We mistake responsibility for sovereignty. And it makes us miserable. We can't relax. We can't sleep. We find no peace. When we believe that we are the "saviors" and that it is all up to us to fix everyone and everything that is broken, it creates a crushing sense of anxiety.

Many people cannot find internal peace because they believe that they are in control. We confuse our ability to make decisions in life with having actual power. Trials and tribulations force us to recognize Allah's irresistible power over us. He is *Al-Qahar* (The Irresistible, the Subduer) and *Al-Azeez* (the All-Mighty). This knowledge then leads to a redeeming understanding of our own poverty and need for Allah. It inspires a beautiful humility before God. It inspires an experiential understanding of the golden statement: "La hawla wa la quwwata illa billah": that there is no change in state and no power or strength, except by Allah. That it is not us that can save anyone or anything. That it is not us who can fix it. That we are *not* in charge. Allah is.

This realization can save our lives. It can save our relationships. The human heart was never created to carry the weight of the world upon it. Only Allah can carry this weight and until we can hand this burden to the One who owns the heavens and the earth, we will continue to suffer under the crushing weight of this false sense of control.

Gaining Sincerity

Another benefit discussed by Sheikh Al-`Izz Ibn`Abdus-Salam is the development of *ikhlas* (purity) within our hearts. When we go through trials, we develop a deeper, experiential level of sincerity. Our desire for the pleasure of people diminishes and our desire for the pleasure of Allah increases and becomes our primary focus. Two of the most deadly spiritual diseases is "hubb ul jaah" (the love of status) and "riyaa" (to show off in worship).

As human beings, we covet the hearts (love, admiration) of people. Depending on our disposition, we seek to attain this love and admiration through different means. If we are not religious, we "collect hearts" by showing off in Dunya (jaah–status). We covet wealth and status symbols to attain the admiration of people.

But, when we are religious, we "collect hearts" using religion. So we show off in matters of worship and deen (religion). This is riyaa (the hidden shirk). The Prophet (pbuh) said:

يَا أَبَا بَكْرٍ، لَلشِّرْكُ فِيكُمْ أَخْفَى مِنْ دَبِيبِ النَّمْلِ، فَقَالَ أَبُو بَكْرٍ: وَهَلِ الشِّرْكُ إِلاَّ مَنْ جَعَلَ مَعَ اللهِ إِلَهًا آخَرَ؟ فَقَالَ النَّبِيُّ صلى الله عليه وسلم: وَالَّذِى نَفْسِى بِيَدِهِ، لَلشِّرْكُ أَخْفَى مِنْ دَبِيبِ النَّمْلِ، أَلاَ أَدُلُّكَ عَلَى شَىْءٍ إِذَا قُلْتَهُ ذَهَبَ عَنْكَ قَلِيلُهُ وَكَثِيرُهُ؟ قَالَ: قُلِ: اللَّهُمَّ إِنِّى أَعُوذُ بِكَ أَنْ أُشْرِكَ بِكَ وَأَنَا أَعْلَمُ، وَأَسْتَغْفِرُكَ لِمَا لاَ أَعْلَمُ

"O Abu Bakr, there is idolatry among you people that is more hidden than the crawling of an ant." Abu Bakr said, 'Is there idolatry other than to make another god alongside Allah?' The Prophet said, 'By one in whose hand is my soul, there is idolatry more hidden than the crawling of an ant. Shall I not tell you something to say to rid you of it both minor and major? Say: O Allah, I seek refuge in you that I associate partners with you while I know, and I seek your forgiveness for what I do not know.'" (Al-Adab al-Mufrad 716, Sahih)

Allah (swt) warned us about this trait in His Book, "So woe to the worshipers, who are neglectful of their prayers, those who only want to be seen (yura'un)." (Quran 107:4-6)

The Prophet (pbuh) also said, "Shall I not inform you of what I fear for you more than the maseeh ud-dajjaal (false messiah)? It is the hidden shirk (riyaa). It is when a man stands up for prayer, then beautifies his prayer for another to look at." (Ibn Majah)

The Messenger of Allah (pbuh) warned us:

"Two hungry wolves roaming freely among a flock of sheep are less destructive than the passion of a man for wealth and high status is to his religion." (Sunan al-Tirmidhī 2376, Sahih)

مَا ذِئْبَانِ جَائِعَانِ أُرْسِلَا فِي غَنَمٍ بِأَفْسَدَ لَهَا مِنْ حِرْصِ الْمَرْءِ عَلَى الْمَالِ وَالشَّرَفِ لِدِينِهِ

Here the Prophet (pbuh) is warning us of two extremely destructive traits: 'hirs' (desperately coveting) of: wealth (maal) and status (sharaf/jaah).

And one of the benefits attained through trials and tribulations is the reorientation of our hearts to seek Allah, rather than people, to seek to be seen, praised, and appreciated by Allah, rather than by people. This is *Ikhlas* (pure sincerity). It's so powerful to reflect on the attributes of Allah that address every one of our needs. In this case, we seek to be seen, and it is Allah who is *Al-Baseer* (The One who sees all). We also seek to be appreciated and He is *Al-Shakur* (The One who appreciates).

The Push to Return (Inaaba)

Another benefit discussed by Sheikh Al-`Izz Ibn`Abdus-Salam is the push to *inaaba*. *Inaaba* is to return to Allah—but not just to return with yourself (tawbah). *Inaaba* is to return to Allah with everything you have (family, career, money, skills, etc.). Prophet Ibraheem (AS) is described as *muneeb* (the one who embodies *inaaba*).

Scholars describe 4 ways that people can become *muneeb (one who re-turns to God with everything)*. The first way that Allah brings us to *inaaba* is through His gifts and love. The second way is ironically as a result of sin that leads the individual to repent in humility and turn back *fully*. The third way that Allah brings us back to Him fully, is by way of our human needs, which push us to seek their fulfillment from Allah. And finally, calamities and tests (bala'a) push us to *inaaba*.

When we witness Allah's might, along with realizing our own poverty–if we are sincere–we will be led to *inaaba*. We will be led to return to Allah completely with all that we have. All of the ingredients of inaaba are triggered and developed by trials and tribulations. And through struggle.

Gaining Understanding of This Temporary Life

Trials and tribulations also lead us to a deep understanding of "inna lilahi wa inna ilayhi rajioon": that indeed we belong to Allah and indeed to Allah we return. This is the deep understanding that, not only do we *control* nothing, but *own* nothing. Everything we have belongs to God. And everything we have, will return to God. This understanding will free us. And allow us to survive the deepest of loss. Our loved ones belong to Allah. Our possessions belong to Allah. Our every ability belongs to Allah. These are gifts from Him. And they return to Him. This is why Allah says in the Quran:

"And We will surely test you with something of fear and hunger and a loss of wealth and lives and fruits, but give good tidings to those who patiently persevere. Those who, when disaster strikes them, say, 'Indeed we belong to God, and indeed to Him we will return.'" (Quran 2:155-156)

وَلَنَبْلُوَنَّكُم بِشَيْءٍ مِّنَ الْخَوْفِ وَالْجُوعِ وَنَقْصٍ مِّنَ الْأَمْوَالِ وَالْأَنفُسِ وَالثَّمَرَاتِ ۗ وَبَشِّرِ الصَّابِرِينَ ۝ الَّذِينَ إِذَا أَصَابَتْهُم مُّصِيبَةٌ قَالُوا إِنَّا لِلَّهِ وَإِنَّا إِلَيْهِ رَاجِعُونَ ۝

This statement is not just words said by the tongue. It is an entire paradigm. It is a way of seeing the world. In this ayah, Allah prepares us for the different kinds of trials which we will experience in this world (fear, hunger, loss). And then He gives glad tidings (bushra) to the ones who have sabr (patient perseverance).

This is amazing because we do not typically hear a person congratulating or giving glad tidings to someone who has just experienced loss or hardship. Allah is saying to give good news to that person. Allah is actually giving glad tidings to the people who have lost something or someone they love. Why? Because those who have sabr are given three priceless gifts. The people of "inna lilahi wa inna ilayhi rajioon" will be gifted with Divine blessings, mercy and guidance:

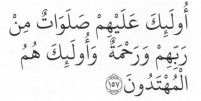

"Those are the ones upon whom are blessings from their Lord and mercy. And it is those who are the [rightly] guided." (Quran 2:157)

Understanding that everything belongs to Allah is the first step to this salvation. Imagine that a very generous friend allows you to borrow their car. And because of their generosity, they allow you to keep that car for 10 years. But imagine that during that decade, you had amnesia and forgot who the car actually belonged to. When that generous friend comes to take their own car back, the one who forgot who it belonged to will respond with anger and resentment. That person might say things like, "How could you do this to me?" "How could you take *my* car?" "It's not fair!"

But why does that happen? This happens because this person forgot who the car actually belonged to. If that person never had amnesia and remembered that the car in fact belonged to the generous friend, then when the friend comes to take it back, what will their response be? "It belongs to you and to you it returns." You might be sad to part with it, but ultimately it is recognized that the friend owns the car. That is what "Inna lillahi wa inna ilaihi raji'oon" means. It is the realization that our spouse, our child, our money, our health, all belong to Allah. They always belonged to Allah and to Allah they return. And responding in this way brings priceless Divine blessings and gifts.

Beloved author, C. S. Lewis addresses a similar concept when he spoke to students at Oxford in October of 1939–less than 2 months after the outbreak of World War II. In his address, he begins by asking how it will be possible for life to continue as usual, "when the lives of our friends and the liberties of Europe are in the balance?" He answers: "The war creates no absolutely new situation: it simply aggravates the permanent human situation so that we can no longer ignore it. Human life has always been lived on the edge of a precipice."

Lewis continues:

"War threatens us with death and pain. No man–and especially no Christian who remembers Gethsemane–need try to attain a stoic indifference about these things: but we can guard against the illusions of the imagination. What does war do to death? It certainly does not make it more frequent; 100 percent of us die, and the percentage cannot be increased…War makes death real to us: and that would have been regarded as one of its blessings by most of the great Christians of the past. They thought it good for us to be always aware of our mortality. I am inclined to think they were right. All the animal life in us, all schemes of happiness that centered in this world, were always doomed to a final frustration. *In ordinary times only a wise man can realize it. Now the stupidest of us know. We see unmistakably the sort of universe in which we have all along been living, and must come to terms with it.*"

Tests In Our Relationships

When we are tested in our relationships, there are several purposes which these types of trials can serve.

SERVICE

When we are given gifts by God, such as knowledge, or any skill or talent, these gifts are also tests. They honor us, but they also place us in a position to help, serve, and save others. If we use these gifts for this purpose, we will be given more by the Giver.

We are also tested in love, when we are gifted (people we love, wealth, status or power). Many people fail in this test when they begin to love the gift more than the Giver. If that happens, the gift itself becomes a barrier, rather than a path, to Allah.

INSPIRATION AND LESSONS FOR OTHERS

We may also be tested through injury. These injuries may or may not be inflicted by the hands of others. But sometimes our response to these injuries serves as a means of saving or inspiring others. For example, some people are brought closer to Allah by observing the heroic or inspiring response of others who have been tested or afflicted. This phenomenon is demonstrated a lot in literature and poetry. For example, there are times when forgiveness can free another person. In his famous novel, *Les Misérables*, Victor Hugo writes about this phenomenon. Hugo describes a convict named Jean Valjean who was forever branded by his past sins; many years prior, he stole a loaf of bread to feed his starving niece. From that day forward, he was known as a thief and could not escape the branding.

One day, a bishop allowed Valjean to stay the night in his home. That night Valjean stole again from the Bishop out of desperation, and tried to escape. The police caught Valjean and returned him to the Bishop's home, along with the silver he had stolen. This was the point when Valjean's life would transform. The bishop was determined to help Jean Valjean see his potential. To do that, it required that Jean Valjean experience forgiveness first. The bishop not only forgave Valjean, he even offered him more silver and said to him, "*Jean Valjean, my brother. You no longer belong to evil. With this silver I bought your soul. I've ransomed you from fear and hatred. And now I give you back to God.*"

From that day forward, Jean Valjean became a different person. He became an honest and honorable man, who went out of his way to help those in need.

Trauma in the Quran

Throughout the Quran, Allah acknowledges the emotional and psychological injuries that we experience in this life. And He speaks about healing those injuries. Allah says:

وَنَزَعْنَا مَا فِي صُدُورِهِمْ مِنْ غِلٍّ تَجْرِي مِنْ تَحْتِهِمُ الْأَنْهَارُ
وَقَالُوا الْحَمْدُ لِلَّهِ الَّذِي هَدَانَا لِهَذَا وَمَا كُنَّا لِنَهْتَدِيَ لَوْلَا
أَنْ هَدَانَا اللَّهُ لَقَدْ جَاءَتْ رُسُلُ رَبِّنَا بِالْحَقِّ وَنُودُوا أَنْ
تِلْكُمُ الْجَنَّةُ أُورِثْتُمُوهَا بِمَا كُنْتُمْ تَعْمَلُونَ ﴿٤٣﴾

"And We shall remove from their hearts any lurking sense of injury (bitterness); beneath them will be rivers flowing. And they will say, 'Praise to Allah, who has guided us to this; and we would never have been guided if Allah had not guided us. Certainly the messengers of our Lord had come with the truth.' And they will be called, 'This is Paradise, which you have been made to inherit for what you used to do.'" (Quran 7:43)

Allah shows us that even the believers may end up carrying the residue of emotional trauma inside their hearts. Surat Al Tawbah is one of the chapters that discusses the trauma which the Prophet (pbuh) and his companions were experiencing at the hands of the disbelievers. In this chapter, Allah talks about removing rage from the hearts of the believers:

"And remove the rage from the believers' hearts. And Allah turns in forgiveness to whom He wills; and Allah is Knowing and Wise." (Quran 9:15)

وَيُذْهِبْ غَيْظَ قُلُوبِهِمْ وَيَتُوبُ اللَّهُ عَلَى مَنْ يَشَاءُ وَاللَّهُ عَلِيمٌ حَكِيمٌ ۝

Allah also gives us many examples in the Quran of the trauma that the Prophets and the righteous experienced throughout their lives. These righteous people were human and felt human emotions. They loved and lost and faced rejection and pain, as we do. Allah uses them as an example to show us how He saves the believer—no matter how dark their situation looks. Studying their stories gives our own hearts strength and resolve. And this is the very reason Allah has told us their stories:

"And each [story] We relate to you from the news of the messengers, that by which We make firm your heart. And there has come to you, in this, the truth and an instruction and a reminder for the believers." (Quran 11:120)

وَكُلًّا نَقُصُّ عَلَيْكَ مِنْ أَنْبَاءِ الرُّسُلِ مَا نُثَبِّتُ بِهِ فُؤَادَكَ وَجَاءَكَ فِي هَذِهِ الْحَقُّ وَمَوْعِظَةٌ وَذِكْرَى لِلْمُؤْمِنِينَ ۝

Maryam (AS) and Ayesha (RA)

Both Maryam (AS), mother of Jesus (AS), and Ayesha (RA), the wife of Prophet Muhammad (pbuh), were wrongly accused of being unchaste. Allah shows us the depth of Maryam's (AS) anguish in the Quran through her words:

"And the pains of childbirth drove her to the trunk of a palm tree. She said, 'Oh, I wish I had died before this and was in oblivion, forgotten.'" (Quran 19:23)

فَأَجَاءَهَا الْمَخَاضُ إِلَى جِذْعِ النَّخْلَةِ قَالَتْ يَا لَيْتَنِي مِتُّ قَبْلَ هَذَا وَكُنْتُ نَسْيًا مَنْسِيًّا ۝

Allah gives us a glimpse into her anguish. Her emotional state. She was in so much pain, both physically and emotionally. But, Allah also shows us how He carried her through. Allah provided for her and gave her comfort and relief. Allah says:

فَنَادَاهَا مِنْ تَحْتِهَا أَلَّا تَحْزَنِي قَدْ جَعَلَ رَبُّكِ تَحْتَكِ سَرِيًّا ۝ وَهُزِّي إِلَيْكِ بِجِذْعِ النَّخْلَةِ تُسَاقِطْ عَلَيْكِ رُطَبًا جَنِيًّا ۝ فَكُلِي وَاشْرَبِي وَقَرِّي عَيْنًا فَإِمَّا تَرَيِنَّ مِنَ الْبَشَرِ أَحَدًا فَقُولِي إِنِّي نَذَرْتُ لِلرَّحْمَنِ صَوْمًا فَلَنْ أُكَلِّمَ الْيَوْمَ إِنْسِيًّا ۝

"But he called her from below her, 'Do not grieve; your Lord has provided beneath you a stream. And shake toward you the trunk of the palm tree; it will drop upon you ripe, fresh dates. So eat and drink and be consoled.' And if you see from among humanity anyone, say, 'Indeed, I have vowed to the Most Merciful abstention, so I will not speak today to [any] man.'" (Quran 19:24-26)

After providing for Maryam (AS) and consoling her, Allah defended her in a way she could not have defended herself–just as He did for Ayesha (RA). Both were wrongly accused, and both were defended and exonerated by God Himself:

$$\text{فَأَتَتْ بِهِ قَوْمَهَا تَحْمِلُهُ ۖ قَالُوا يَا مَرْيَمُ لَقَدْ جِئْتِ شَيْئًا}$$
$$\text{فَرِيًّا ۝ يَا أُخْتَ هَارُونَ مَا كَانَ أَبُوكِ امْرَأَ سَوْءٍ وَمَا}$$
$$\text{كَانَتْ أُمُّكِ بَغِيًّا ۝ فَأَشَارَتْ إِلَيْهِ ۖ قَالُوا كَيْفَ نُكَلِّمُ مَنْ}$$
$$\text{كَانَ فِي الْمَهْدِ صَبِيًّا ۝ قَالَ إِنِّي عَبْدُ اللَّهِ آتَانِيَ الْكِتَابَ}$$
$$\text{وَجَعَلَنِي نَبِيًّا ۝}$$

"Then she brought him to her people, carrying him. They said, 'O Mary, you have certainly done a thing unprecedented. Oh sister of Aaron, your father was not a man of evil, nor was your mother unchaste.' So she pointed to him. They said, 'How can we speak to one who is in the cradle, a child?' [Jesus] said, 'Indeed, I am the servant of Allah. He has given me the Scripture and made me a Prophet.'" (Quran 19:27-30)

Allah told Maryam (AS) not to speak. Her own means could have done nothing for her. When Ayesha (RA) was falsely accused of infidelity, she reported the same: she thought no one would believe her–even in her denial. We are shown both of their anguish.

And then we are shown how Allah carried and saved them both.

Mother of Musa (AS)

Allah describes the trauma of the mother of Musa (AS):

"And the heart of Moses' mother became empty [of all else]. She was about to disclose [the matter concerning] him had We not bound fast her heart, that she would be of the believers." (Quran 28:10)

$$\text{وَأَصْبَحَ فُؤَادُ أُمِّ مُوسَى}$$
$$\text{فَارِغًا ۖ إِنْ كَادَتْ لَتُبْدِي بِهِ}$$
$$\text{لَوْلَا أَنْ رَبَطْنَا عَلَى قَلْبِهَا}$$
$$\text{لِتَكُونَ مِنَ الْمُؤْمِنِينَ ۝}$$

Allah first tells us about the state that the mother of Musa (AS) was in. Allah says that "her heart was empty" after she had to part from her child. But then Allah also says how He literally "held her heart together" (rabatna ala qalbiha). She was suffering due to the separation from her son. But Allah took care of her heart. Many of us have had to be separated from those we love. Grief hits us all. But it is Allah who holds the heart together. Go to Allah to tie your heart together. Go to Allah to bring the broken pieces together to make it whole and even more beautiful than it was before. Like the broken pottery that the Japanese turn into art (kintsugi). Allah can bring the pieces of your heart together and mend it with gold. Just as He did with the heart of Musa's mother.

After holding her heart together, Allah returned her child to her. And Allah has promised that the believer will always be reunited with their lost loved ones–in this life or the next:

"Thus did We return Moses to his mother so that she would be comforted and would not grieve. And so she would know that the promise of God is true. But most people do not know." (Quran 28:13)

فَرَدَدْنَاهُ إِلَى أُمِّهِ كَيْ تَقَرَّ عَيْنُهَا وَلَا تَحْزَنَ وَلِتَعْلَمَ أَنَّ وَعْدَ اللَّهِ حَقٌّ وَلَكِنَّ أَكْثَرَهُمْ لَا يَعْلَمُونَ ۝

Grief and Prophet Muhammad (pbuh)

The Quran often addresses the *grief and sadness* of Prophet Muhammad (pbuh). Allah says:

"Then perhaps you would kill yourself through grief over them, [O Muhammad], if they do not believe in this message, [and] out of sorrow." (Quran 18:6)

فَلَعَلَّكَ بَاخِعٌ نَفْسَكَ عَلَى آثَارِهِمْ إِنْ لَمْ يُؤْمِنُوا بِهَذَا الْحَدِيثِ أَسَفًا ۝

The Prophet Muhammad (pbuh) went through a great deal of trauma throughout his life. Before he was born, his father died, and as a child, his mother died, followed by the grandfather who cared for him. He experienced abuse at the hands of his own people and even his own family. In the course of his life, he lost many companions, his beloved wife Khadijah (RA) and his uncle who supported him. Before he died, he had buried every single one of his children, except one.

Throughout the Quran, Allah addresses the pain of the Prophet (pbuh) and we see how Allah gives him counsel. Allah heals the hearts by acknowledging our pain, confirming that we are seen and understood, and reassuring us that abuse is not our fault, and that no one can dishonor or degrade us because all honor belongs only to Allah.

COUNSEL THROUGH ACKNOWLEDGMENT

In this ayah, Allah gives comfort through *acknowledging* the pain:

"And We already know that your chest is constrained by what they say." (Quran 15:97)

وَلَقَدْ نَعْلَمُ أَنَّكَ يَضِيقُ صَدْرُكَ بِمَا يَقُولُونَ ٩٧

COUNSEL THROUGH BEING SEEN AND UNDERSTOOD

In this ayah, Allah provides comfort by confirming that He *knows* and *understands* what he's going through:

"So let not their speech grieve you. Indeed, We know what they conceal and what they declare." (Quran 36:76)

فَلَا يَحْزُنْكَ قَوْلُهُمْ إِنَّا نَعْلَمُ مَا يُسِرُّونَ وَمَا يُعْلِنُونَ ٧٦

COUNSEL THROUGH REASSURANCE THAT THE VICTIM IS NOT TO BLAME

In this ayah, Allah comforts the Prophet (pbuh) by reassuring him that the abuse he experienced was not his fault or because of something *in him*.

"We know that you, [O Muhammad], are saddened by what they say. But indeed, it is not you that they reject, but it is the verses of Allah that the wrongdoers reject." (Quran 6:33)

قَدْ نَعْلَمُ إِنَّهُ لَيَحْزُنُكَ الَّذِى يَقُولُونَ فَإِنَّهُمْ لَا يُكَذِّبُونَكَ وَلَـٰكِنَّ الظَّالِمِينَ بِآيَاتِ اللَّهِ يَجْحَدُونَ ٣٣

COUNSEL THROUGH REASSURANCE ABOUT DIGNITY

In this ayah, Allah provides comfort in knowing that all Honor comes only from Allah. And that no one has the power to dishonor you or take away your dignity because all honor and dignity belong to Allah:

"And let not their speech grieve you. Indeed, honor [due to power] belongs to Allah entirely. He is the Hearing, the Knowing." (Quran 10:65)

وَلَا يَحْزُنْكَ قَوْلُهُمْ إِنَّ الْعِزَّةَ لِلَّهِ جَمِيعًا هُوَ السَّمِيعُ الْعَلِيمُ ٦٥

It is essential to remember that Allah tells us these stories because they apply to *us, to our pain, to our trauma*. And through the comfort that Allah is giving to His Prophet (pbuh), Allah also comforts and heals us.

Fear and Prophet Musa (AS)

Another Prophet that the Quran speaks about at length is Prophet Musa (AS). Musa (AS) also experienced great trauma. He was born at a time when baby boys were killed by the Pharoah, as a political policy. He had to be separated from his mother, but was later reunited as a mercy from God. Then as an adult he accidentally killed a man and had to flee for his life from the oppressive Pharaoh. When he escaped, he had no one and nothing with him, except the help of Allah.

The Quran often addresses and heals the *fear* of Prophet Musa (AS). Allah says:

"And he became inside the city fearful and vigilant when suddenly the one who sought his help the previous day cried out to him [once again]. Moses said to him, 'Indeed, you are an evident, [persistent] deviator.'" (Quran 28:18)	فَأَصْبَحَ فِي الْمَدِينَةِ خَائِفًا يَتَرَقَّبُ فَإِذَا الَّذِى اسْتَنصَرَهُ بِالْأَمْسِ يَسْتَصْرِخُهُ قَالَ لَهُ مُوسَى إِنَّكَ لَغَوِيٌّ مُّبِينٌ ﴿١٨﴾

After all the trauma Musa (AS) experienced at the hands of Pharaoh, Musa (AS) was given the heavy task of facing the oppressor himself. Before taking on this heavy mission, Musa (AS) made a very powerful duaa.

He said,

"[Moses] said, 'My Lord, expand for me my breast. And make my task easy for me.'" (Quran 20: 25-26)	قَالَ رَبِّ اشْرَحْ لِي صَدْرِى ﴿٢٥﴾ وَيَسِّرْ لِي أَمْرِى ﴿٢٦﴾

It is so profound to reflect on this duaa. Musa (AS) was tasked with such a difficult job. Pharaoh was the tyrant who killed and enslaved Musa's (AS) people. And now he had the traumatizing job of addressing him. Face to face. So what does Musa (AS) ask for? He asks Allah to *expand his chest* and ease his task. This is deep. Expansion does not remove the hardship itself. It does not make the obstacle disappear. *Expansion shrinks the obstacle.* It *eases* the hardship. Musa's (AS) duaa did not make Pharoah disappear. It did not make his task go away. Granting his duaa gave Musa (AS) expansion, which eased his task and carried him through.

So often we wish that our fears and our grief and all our problems could just disappear. But this life is not jannah (paradise). This life is inherently imperfect. No matter how much money, power, beauty, status someone has, their life will never be perfect. There will always be some fear. There will always be some grief. Some loss. Some pain. There will always be storms. But there is a way to navigate those storms.

Our hearts were made vulnerable in this life; but this is not a *mistake* in the Design. It is part of the Divine Design that we will experience emotional and psychological wounds. It is part of our growth and purification. It is part of our development, on our journey back to God. So, if our wounds are designed as part of this journey, it is essential to have a deep understanding of healing. The four essential steps to healing are: diagnosing the root cause of our pain, removing the barriers to healing, treating the wound, and then guarding the heart.

Diagnosing the Suffering

Diagnosing the Root of Our Suffering

We will bleed in this life. We will get hurt sometimes. And our heart will break. But there is a way to heal and always come back stronger and even more beautiful. The first step to healing is: diagnosing the root cause of our pain. Allah says,

لَهُ مُعَقِّبَاتٌ مِنْ بَيْنِ يَدَيْهِ وَمِنْ خَلْفِهِ يَحْفَظُونَهُ مِنْ أَمْرِ اللَّهِ إِنَّ اللَّهَ لَا يُغَيِّرُ مَا بِقَوْمٍ حَتَّى يُغَيِّرُوا مَا بِأَنْفُسِهِمْ وَإِذَا أَرَادَ اللَّهُ بِقَوْمٍ سُوءًا فَلَا مَرَدَّ لَهُ وَمَا لَهُمْ مِنْ دُونِهِ مِنْ وَالٍ ﴿١١﴾

"Indeed Allah does not change the condition of a people, until they change what is inside themselves." (Quran 13:11).

We all understand what happens if we get a physical wound. We understand that it needs treatment, and we need to go to a doctor. We know there needs to be a process for that wound to recover. Unfortunately, when someone has an emotional or psychological wound, many people do not have this same understanding. There is often very little patience or compassion for the process necessary for healing. Instead there is the notion that people can "just get over it" or "suck it up". And yet, no one would tell a person who broke their leg, to just "walk it off". No one would say that if they just had enough iman (faith) and sabr (patience), they wouldn't need to go to the doctor or get a cast and crutches. There is a completely different standard when it comes to dealing with emotional and psychological wounds. Many of us lack the resources and the support to do what is necessary for healing. What would happen if we covered a gunshot wound with a bandage and just assumed that "time would heal all wounds"? That wound would not go away just because it was covered up. In fact, time would make an untreated wound worse. It would become infected and harm the rest of the body as well.

Many of us engage in these types of avoidant coping behaviors to treat our emotional wounds. We live in a social media culture where perfection is demanded and put on display. As a result, many people who are suffering from deep, often old, emotional traumas spend a great deal of effort trying to hold up a mask for the world. But the project of appearing perfect to the world, on social media and beyond, is an exhausting one. It uses up all the energy we could otherwise use to actually address and heal our pain. Many people spend years putting bandages on gunshot wounds. Some people go to fantastic lengths "decorating" those bandages so the world will believe that they are perfect, that their lives are perfect, that their families are perfect. And social media provides a perfect platform for this charade. But who suffers most? The person with the wound does. Unhealed trauma will affect everything–until it is healed.

Four Elements of the Human Being

The process of diagnosing the root cause of our pain involves a deep look at the different elements that make up the human being. In order to discover the underlying cause of our suffering, we need to understand that human beings are complex. We are not only a physical body. The human being has four elements: biological, psychological, environmental, and spiritual. Each of these elements have needs that must be fulfilled in order for a human to be holistically healthy and happy.

Biological

The biological element of the human being consists of our body, organics, chemicals, hormones, and neurotransmitters like dopamine and serotonin. There can be a breakdown in this element, which will lead to pain and ultimately to suffering, if the pain is not addressed. For example, a breakdown in the thyroid can lead to debilitating depression, and lack of energy. The biological element of the human being requires oxygen, food, water, and if there is a deprivation, it must be filled. The organs, chemicals, hormones, etc. need to be functioning correctly and if there is a malfunction, it must be fixed.

The conventional approach to depression often focuses only on the biological element of the human being–and only a subcategory of it. People who suffer from severe emotional and psychological pain, such as depression and anxiety, are often told it is simply due to a chemical imbalance of the brain. While chemical imbalances do exist, this explanation is only a tiny part of the story. For example, one Harvard study by Dr. Irving Kirsch found that just improving sleep patterns improves depression by 6 points on the Hamilton Scale, while chemical antidepressants give an improvement of only 1.8 on average.

This is not to say chemical imbalances do not exist; but often the approach is highly myopic. Even within the biological sphere, there are many other factors that can contribute to depression such as: bad diet, leaky gut, sleep disorders, postpartum changes, hypothyroidism, low vitamin D and low B-12.

And yet, many "treatments" simply treat the human being like a physical machine with a broken piece. Patients are often told that they have a malfunctioning brain that is not producing the right chemicals. The conventional biological approach to mental health often only looks at this one element of the human being and thereby often misses other possible root causes for the pain. This myopic approach often only treats or numbs the symptoms of the emotional pain, without treating the root cause.

Psychological/Cognitive

The psychological or cognitive element of the human being refers to the way we think, our thought patterns, attributional styles, and mental schemas about the world. In other words, this is the way we view ourselves and the world, and the way we process the world around us. This element must be healthy, or it will cause us great pain and suffering.

According to world renowned physician and trauma expert, Dr. Gabor Maté, there is a direct connection between mind and body health. He has authored several books exploring issues related to ADHD, stress, developmental psychology, and addiction. He demonstrates that emotional stress is a major cause of physical illness, from cancer to autoimmune conditions and many other chronic diseases. The brain and body systems that process emotions are intimately connected to the hormonal apparatus, the nervous system, and in particular the immune system. Dr. Maté's insights into the relationship of the mind and the body are presented in his book: *When the Body Says No*.

Trauma can be understood as a "relational" term, a concept that connects an outer occurrence with its specific consequences for an inner psychic reality. According to Professor Arnold Cooper at the University of Wisconsin–Madison, psychic trauma is any psychological event that abruptly overwhelms the capacity to *"provide a minimal sense of safety and integrative intactness, resulting in overwhelming anxiety or helplessness, or the threat of it, and producing an enduring change in the psychic organization."*

Unhealed trauma often leads to unhealthy cognitive patterns and self-concepts. Like any physical wound, emotional wounds need to be treated and healed in order to avoid further pain and disease.

ATTRIBUTIONAL STYLES

Healing the way we think may require therapy, which helps us replace negative thought patterns, schemas, and attributional styles, with positive ones. For example, the research of top psychologists Seligman, Abramson and others, finds that people with negative attributional styles (internal, stable, global) are more likely to suffer from depression. For example, an investigation into post-transplant patients found that an optimistic explanatory style was more significantly associated with higher quality of life than age and gender. Put simply, when an *uncontrollable* negative event occurs, individuals with a negative attributional style will internalize blame (internal), will believe that the cause of the negative experience/state will never improve (stable), and will think that the negative event will affect every aspect of their life (global). When a positive event happens, individuals with a negative attributional style will reverse the causal attributions (external, unstable, local). They will view positive events as temporary and due to just "luck" (external). They will believe that positive occurrences are just temporary (unstable) and that the positive occurrence is limited in scope (local). These types of maladaptive thought patterns can fuel depression by creating a cycle of negative thought that perpetuates the problem.

Individuals with a positive attributional style (external, unstable, local) will process uncontrollable negative life experiences very differently. When they experience an uncontrollable negative event, they do *not* internalize blame (external). They believe that the negative experience/state is temporary (unstable) and that it does not extend to every aspect of their life (local). An optimistic explanatory style is associated with higher levels of motivation, achievement, and physical well-being, as well as lower levels of depressive symptoms. For example, studies conducted by Nolen-Hoeksema, Girgus, and Seligman, with middle-school children showed that re-training pessimistic thinking into optimistic thinking can significantly reduce the incidence of depression.

ISLAMIC ATTRIBUTIONAL STYLES

When we examine the worldview presented in the Quran and sunnah, we discover this positive attributional style throughout the text.

External

We are taught by Allah and His messenger (pbuh) that there are some events which are not in our control, and therefore, we cannot and should not internalize blame. The belief in Qadr (Divine Destiny) is a pillar of our faith. Allah says:

مَا أَصَابَ مِنْ مُصِيبَةٍ فِي الْأَرْضِ وَلَا فِي أَنْفُسِكُمْ إِلَّا فِي كِتَابٍ مِنْ قَبْلِ أَنْ نَبْرَأَهَا إِنَّ ذَلِكَ عَلَى اللَّهِ يَسِيرٌ ﴿٢٢﴾ لِكَيْلَا تَأْسَوْا عَلَى مَا فَاتَكُمْ وَلَا تَفْرَحُوا بِمَا آتَاكُمْ وَاللَّهُ لَا يُحِبُّ كُلَّ مُخْتَالٍ فَخُورٍ ﴿٢٣﴾

"No disaster strikes upon the earth or among yourselves except that it is in a register before We bring it into being – indeed that is easy for Allah. In order that you do not despair over what has passed you by, and not exult [in pride] over what He has given you. And Allah does not like anyone, self-deluded and boastful." (Quran 57:22-23)

The Prophet (pbuh) said:

احْفَظِ اللَّهَ تَجِدْهُ أَمَامَكَ تَعَرَّفْ إِلَى اللَّهِ فِي الرَّخَاءِ يَعْرِفْكَ فِي الشِّدَّةِ وَاعْلَمْ أَنَّ مَا أَخْطَأَكَ لَمْ يَكُنْ لِيُصِيبَكَ وَمَا أَصَابَكَ لَمْ يَكُنْ لِيُخْطِئَكَ وَاعْلَمْ أَنَّ النَّصْرَ مَعَ الصَّبْرِ وَأَنَّ الْفَرَجَ مَعَ الْكَرْبِ وَأَنَّ مَعَ الْعُسْرِ يُسْرًا

"Be mindful of Allah, you will find him in front of you. Know Allah during times of prosperity, He will know you in times of adversity. **Know that what has passed you by was never to befall you. And [know that] what has befallen you was never to have passed you by.** *And know that victory accompanies perseverance, relief accompanies affliction and ease accompanies hardship."* (Hadith 19 of 40 Hadith An-Nawawi)

In another narration, the Prophet (pbuh) said:

عَنْ عَبْدِ اللَّهِ بْنِ عَبَّاسٍ رَضِيَ اللَّهُ عَنْهُمَا قَالَ كُنْت خَلْفَ رَسُولِ اللَّهِ صلى الله عليه و سلم يَوْمًا فَقَالَ يَا غُلَامُ إِنِّي أُعَلِّمُك كَلِمَاتٍ احْفَظْ اللَّهَ يَحْفَظْك احْفَظْ اللَّهَ تَجِدْهُ تُجَاهَك إِذَا سَأَلْت فَاسْأَلْ اللَّهَ وَإِذَا اسْتَعَنْت فَاسْتَعِنْ بِاللَّهِ وَاعْلَمْ أَنَّ الْأُمَّةَ لَوْ اجْتَمَعَتْ عَلَى أَنْ يَنْفَعُوك بِشَيْءٍ لَمْ يَنْفَعُوك إِلَّا بِشَيْءٍ قَدْ كَتَبَهُ اللَّهُ لَك وَإِنْ اجْتَمَعُوا عَلَى أَنْ يَضُرُّوك بِشَيْءٍ لَمْ يَضُرُّوك إِلَّا بِشَيْءٍ قَدْ كَتَبَهُ اللَّهُ عَلَيْك رُفِعَتْ الْأَقْلَامُ وَجَفَّتْ الصُّحُفُ

"Be mindful of Allah and He will protect you. Be mindful of Allah and you will find Him at your side. If you ask, ask of God. If you need help, seek it from God. Know that if the whole world were to gather together in order to help you; they would not be able to help you except if God had written so. And if the whole world were to gather together in order to harm you; they would not harm you except if God had written so. The pens have been lifted, and the pages have dried." (At-Tirmidhi 2516)

Regarding Allah's Decree (Qadr), the Prophet (pbuh) is saying:

"The Pens have been lifted and the pages have dried." (At-Tirmidhi 2516)	رُفِعَتِ الْأَقْلَامُ وَجَفَّتِ الصُّحُفُ رَوَاهُ التِّرْمِذِيُّ

Truly understanding that the uncontrollable events of our life are exactly that–*not in our control*–allows the believer to find peace in hard times.

Unstable

When something negative happens, we are taught by Allah and His messenger (pbuh) to have hope that things will change for the better. And this is something amazing about studying the Quran. When you read or hear about just one story, you might think, "That doesn't apply to me". But when you widen the lens and you look at the big picture, the powerful collage of stories and experiences that our great heroes of the past went through, you realize something profound. You realize that you can always find yourself in their stories. Every single one of us can find ourselves in their stories.

When we look deeply, we see that Allah does not tell us every aspect of their lives. But there is one particular aspect of every single story that Allah allows us to see. Allah always shows us a glimpse into the very hardest time of each of their lives. And how they reacted.

And how they got through.

Maryam (AS) was a single mother rejected by her own people. Yusuf (AS) was sold into slavery and falsely imprisoned after being thrown into a well by his own brothers. Asiyah (AS) was married to an abusive man who had her tortured. Nuh (AS) had a son who refused to believe and drowned in front of his eyes. Ayesha (RA) was slandered. Ibrahim (AS) had a father who made idols and his people tried to kill him. Lut (AS) was married to a woman who disbelieved and betrayed him. Adam's (AS) son was so jealous, he murdered his other son. Yaqoob (AS) lost his son and cried until he went blind. The mother of Musa (AS) was forced to give up her son to save him from the tyrannical Pharoah. Ayoub (AS) was tested with sickness and financial hardship. Yunus (AS) was trapped in the belly of the fish. Musa (AS) was a fugitive who had to face an extreme oppressor. Muhammad (pbuh) was an orphan who lost his wife and every single one of his children, but one.

These heroes knew grief. They knew pain. And they knew loss.

This is so important because it serves as a sign and lesson for us. This is the part that every one of us share in common with these heroes. They were tested. And we are tested. They felt pain, rejection, defeat. They felt disappointment. They experienced loss. They were hurt by those closest to them. Sometimes their own children (Nuh). Sometimes their own spouse (Lut). Sometimes their own parents (Ibrahim). Yunus (AS) felt trapped. Nuh (AS) felt defeated. Yaqoob (AS) felt grief. They were the greatest creations, and they were human.

So we never need to feel alone in our stories or our own tragedies. Allah has given us their stories to find comfort and inspiration. Because just as Allah shows us their pain and their trials, He also shows us their salvation.

Allah showed us their trials in order to show us their triumph—despite their circumstances. Maryam (AS) was honored as one of the most perfect women and she became the mother of a great Prophet who miraculously defended her. Yusuf (AS) went from being a slave and prisoner, to becoming the Minister of the land and was reunited with his father and brothers. Asiyah (AS) was shown her special home in Paradise, even while she lived. And then she was honored as one of the most perfect women. Nuh (AS) was miraculously saved, along with his people, from the Great Flood. Ibrahim (AS) was saved, even in the midst of the flames when Allah commanded the fire to be cool and a place of *safety* for him. Lut (AS) and his people were saved from the Great Calamity. Adam (AS) became a Prophet and the Father of mankind. Yaqoob (AS) was reunited with both his sons. The mother of Musa (AS) was reunited with her child. Ayoub (AS) was given back his health and wealth and family, and more as a mercy from Allah. Yunus (AS) was saved from the fish and his people believed and were saved. Allah split the Sea for Musa (AS) and saved him from the Pharoah. Muhammad (pbuh) became the Beloved of God and the Seal of the Prophets.

They all went through life's hardships. And they were all saved.

Local

The local attributional style is positive because it is the understanding that when difficulties happen, they are only limited in their scope. For example, if your trial is in the realm of a relationship, people who have a local attributional style will see that the difficulty does not extend to every relationship or other aspects of their life (such as their career, finances or health). Such individuals have a broad perspective and do not allow a challenge in one aspect of their life to overtake all other aspects of their life. It is to keep perspective and widen the lens through which they process their life and experiences. This principle is deeply Islamic. Allah tells us in the Quran, "Verily *with* hardship comes ease." (Quran 94:5)

Ease does not only come *after* the hardship. Ease and blessings are always there, *alongside* the hardship as well. We may be tested in one aspect of our lives, but *at the same time*, Allah has given us countless blessings and ease in other aspects of our lives. *With* the hardship is ease.

WASWASA (WHISPERS) AND THINKING PATTERNS

As believers, we know that Shaytan (Satan) can also influence our thoughts. The process of *waswasa* (whispering) can have a profound effect on how we think and see the world. For example, when a person makes a mistake, Shaytan will try to drown them in shame. He will attempt to paralyze the person with thoughts of worthlessness and despair.

We are taught in the Quran to seek refuge from the whispers of Shaytan. Allahs says:

قُلْ أَعُوذُ بِرَبِّ النَّاسِ ۝ مَلِكِ النَّاسِ ۝ إِلَهِ النَّاسِ ۝ مِنْ شَرِّ الْوَسْوَاسِ الْخَنَّاسِ ۝ الَّذِى يُوَسْوِسُ فِى صُدُورِ النَّاسِ ۝ مِنَ الْجِنَّةِ وَالنَّاسِ ۝

"Say, 'I seek refuge in the Lord of mankind, the Sovereign of mankind, the God of mankind, from the evil of the one who whispers and then retreats (after his whisper), who whispers [evil] into the breasts of mankind. From among the Jinn and human beings.'" (Quran 114:1-6)

Shaytan spends his existence trying to deceive us and take us away from the straight path. And he uses a particular satanic method to do so. He will whisper an evil thought and then he will hide, so that you will believe that it was from you. So that you think it was *your* belief, *your* opinion, *your* idea. Many of us are walking around with thoughts and opinions and beliefs that were actually planted there by Shaytan, but we think they are ours. And sometimes we end up absorbing these deceptive thoughts so deeply that they even become part of our perceived "identity".

Allah shows us Shaytan's chilling confession on the Day of Judgment, after it's too late:

وَقَالَ الشَّيْطَانُ لَمَّا قُضِيَ الْأَمْرُ إِنَّ اللَّهَ وَعَدَكُمْ وَعْدَ
الْحَقِّ وَوَعَدتُّكُمْ فَأَخْلَفْتُكُمْ وَمَا كَانَ لِيَ عَلَيْكُم مِّن
سُلْطَانٍ إِلَّا أَن دَعَوْتُكُمْ فَاسْتَجَبْتُمْ لِي فَلَا تَلُومُونِي
وَلُومُوا أَنفُسَكُم مَّا أَنَا بِمُصْرِخِكُمْ وَمَا أَنتُم بِمُصْرِخِيَّ
إِنِّي كَفَرْتُ بِمَا أَشْرَكْتُمُونِ مِن قَبْلُ إِنَّ الظَّالِمِينَ لَهُمْ
عَذَابٌ أَلِيمٌ ﴿٢٢﴾

*"And Satan will say, when the matter has been concluded, 'Indeed,
Allah had promised you the promise of Truth. And I promised you, but
I betrayed you. But I had no authority over you, except that I invited
you, and you responded to me. So do not blame me; but blame yourselves.
I cannot be called to your aid, nor can you be called to my aid. Indeed,
I deny your association of me [with Allah] before. Indeed, for the
wrongdoers is a painful punishment.'" (Quran 14:22)*

Shaytan Uses Despair

When a believer commits a sin, Shaytan wants to make them feel so unworthy that he/she stops trying to get closer to Allah. Shaytan will use false thoughts like: "You are so bad; you might as well take off your hijab" or "You just committed this sin and now you're going to go pray or go to the masjid? You're a hypocrite!"

By making people believe that they are unworthy of forgiveness or nearness to God, Shaytan uses shame as one of his favorite weapons.

To heal and protect from the onslaught of Shaytan's deception, we must realize that every human being is imperfect and flawed by Divine design. God did not create us perfect, so how could He expect perfection from us? Allah only wants us to keep turning back to Him and renewing ourselves and our hearts through tawbah (returning to God) and istighfar (repentance). Armed with this healthy understanding of God's mercy and forgiveness, the individual can overcome this mental onslaught of Shaytan.

Protection

We are taught that the remembrance of Allah (Thikr, Quran, Salah), acts as a shield from the whispers of Shaytan. For example, the Prophet (pbuh) said: "Whoever recites لَا إِلَهَ إِلَّا اللهُ، وَحْدَهُ لَا شَرِيكَ لَهُ، لَهُ الْمُلْكُ وَلَهُ الْحَمْدُ، وَهُوَ عَلَى كُلِّ شَيْءٍ قَدِيرٌ. ("La ilaha illallahu wahdahu la sharika lahu lahul mulku wa lahul hamdu wa huwa 'ala kulli shay in qadir: "There is nothing worthy of worship but God, alone with no partner, to Him belongs the Dominion, and to Him belongs all the Praise, and He is over all things able.") 100 times in the day, will receive the reward of freeing 10 slaves, 100 rewards will be written for him and 100 sins wiped away, and he will be protected from Shaytan for the remainder of the day." (Sahih Bukhari, Hadith: 3293 and Sahih Muslim, Hadith: 2691)

Environmental

The environmental element refers to our social circle, the conditions we live in, work in, and spend time in. It includes the people around us and the habits we form, such as diet and sleep routines. A healthy environment is an essential part of overall well-being. Sometimes we treat a person's symptoms as though the *person* is broken, when in fact it is their *environment* that is broken. An abusive home/relationship is toxic to a person's emotional and spiritual health.

Sometimes the poison from our environment, may even be from the past. Childhood abuse/neglect can leave a scar that affects us well into adulthood. A German study conducted at the University of Kassel found that more than 75 percent of participants suffering from chronic depression reported clinically significant histories of childhood trauma. Like a wound that has never been treated, even a *past* toxic environment may leave a wound that requires healing through therapy. And this wound must be healed in order for the individual to be emotionally, spiritually, and physically healthy.

Spiritual

The spiritual element of the human being refers to the qalb (spiritual heart) and ruh (soul). This is the eternal part of the human being–the part that will move on to the grave and the afterlife. This part of the human being has essential needs, and if those needs are neglected, the human suffers great pain. The heart and soul require spiritual oxygen and food. The heart and soul also require cleansing and protection. Just like the body.

UNSEEN

A key element of the spiritual realm that can affect a person's state is the unseen. Within the unseen is Shaytan, ayn (evil eye), hassad (envy), and sihr(sourcery). The remembrance of Allah (thikr) is both the protection and the cure for all matters of the unseen.

Allah says,

قُلْ أَعُوذُ بِرَبِّ الْفَلَقِ ۝ مِنْ شَرِّ مَا خَلَقَ ۝ وَمِنْ شَرِّ غَاسِقٍ إِذَا وَقَبَ ۝ وَمِنْ شَرِّ النَّفَّاثَاتِ فِي الْعُقَدِ ۝ وَمِنْ شَرِّ حَاسِدٍ إِذَا حَسَدَ ۝

"Say, 'I seek refuge in the Lord of daybreak. From the evil of that which He created. And from the evil of darkness when it settles. And from the evil of the blowers in knots. And from the evil of an envier when he envies.'" (Quran 113:1-5)

Like the physical elements of human life, the unseen elements can also cause harm without the protection and healing of Allah.

Diagnosing the Root Cause Means Examining All 4 Elements

When something goes wrong in the human being (someone is in severe emotional or psychological pain), we need to search for the cause in all four elements (biological, psychological, environmental, and spiritual). A breakdown in any one of these categories, will cause pain in the human being. That pain is intended as an alarm to alert the human being to a breakdown in that aspect of their being.

If that pain is ignored, it turns into suffering.

For example, when a person suffers from depression or anxiety, we need to examine all 4 of these elements for the root cause of the pain. If we only look at the biological element, we will have ignored 3 out of 4 of the human elements. And therefore our approach will not be complete. If the breakdown is in one or more of the other 3 elements, we may end up only masking the symptoms or numbing the pain through medication and other means. But we would have failed to recognize or heal the true cause of the pain.

Case Studies

Sara

Take for example Sara. She has been in an abusive relationship for the last 10 years. And as a result of the abuse, Sara suffers from debilitating depression and anxiety. When she went to the doctor, she was given antidepressants along with medication for her anxiety. While the drugs did help with her symptoms, have they addressed the root cause of her problem: an abusive environment? No. Instead, she continues to live in that toxic home, while simply numbing the pain.

Ahmed

Consider the example of Ahmed. He has been suffering from depression for the last 6 months. His friends and family want to help, so they tell him that if his faith was stronger, he would "never feel sad". Ahmed is a practicing Muslim who prays regularly and has strong faith. So he can't understand why he's still depressed. The reality is that, while his family means well, their advice is incomplete. They have focused on a crucial element of the human being (the spiritual). But Ahmed is not only a soul. He is also a body. After running some blood tests, Ahmed finds out that his thyroid is underactive and is causing his depression.

Lina

Lina has a great job, a loving husband and a supportive family. She has a beautiful home and two adorable children. Her family is well known and highly respected in the community. They are often busy with social gatherings and have the privilege of taking lavish vacations several times a year. She is healthy and confident. Lina has "everything".

But she still feels empty. And she can't understand why.

Lina is "thriving" in all of the human elements—except one. Lina doesn't pray. She doesn't remember Allah or her meeting with Him. She is culturally Muslim, but her faith plays almost no part in her day-to-day life. So while she may be physically, mentally, and socially "healthy", Lina is spiritually starved. And that spiritual vacancy is the root cause of her pain, despite having everything she wants.

Yusuf

Yusuf has a great job and a loving family. He makes good money, is respected by his colleagues and his community. Yusuf is living the life he always dreamed of. But Yusuf suffers from debilitating depression and intrusive thoughts. What many people do not know about Yusuf, is that he was abused and bullied as a child. As a result of the abuse, Yusuf came to believe that he was not worthy of love and respect. He spends much of his day drowning in self-hatred and negative self-talk. Yusuf was prescribed medication, but it didn't heal his past trauma, nor did it teach him healthier ways to think about himself and his world.

Keep in mind, a breakdown can occur in more than one of the four elements, and all the elements are connected. A breakdown in one realm often leads to a breakdown in other realms. For example, studies show that childhood abuse leads to biological changes in the structure of the brain, which makes a person more susceptible to depression, anxiety and addiction later in life. Or for example, a breakdown in our spirituality will also cause our thought patterns and cognition to be unhealthy. The spiritual heart is the apparatus and lens by which we "see" and *process* the world.

After we have examined all four elements of the human being and diagnosed where the deficiency has occurred, we must move to step two, which is to remove the barriers that impede healing.

STEP TWO:

Removing
Barriers to
Healing

Barrier 1:
Toxic Myths of Sabr

As with any wound, there are factors that assist healing and factors that impede healing. For example, putting dirt in a wound or exposing it to bacteria will delay or block the healing process. In order to move forward, we must remove these barriers, found inside and outside ourselves. Taking an honest look inside ourselves, inside our lives, and our habits, is extremely difficult. But that is the only way we can free ourselves from the flames. In fact, many of us live our entire lives in chains, just because we are terrified of change. We continue to live in chains, but numb the pain of those chains through distractions and sedatives. We hide not only from others; we hide even from ourselves. We quiet the smoke alarm, but sit still in a burning home.

And tragically, we are often *taught* to do just this.

One of the factors that impede healing are our false, toxic, definitions of 'sabr' (patience). The two most common myths about "sabr" are: that sabr means being *stoic* and that sabr means being *passive*.

The Myth of Sabr as
Being Stoic without Tears

One of the most common myths about sabr is the idea that it means feeling (or showing) no emotion. This is the false notion that sabr means being robotic. For example, imagine that two members of a family attend a funeral and one person is crying, while the other person is showing no emotion. Many of us would advise the person crying to have "sabr", while praising the person without emotion for their "great sabr". But this definition is essentially flawed. Sabr does not mean showing or feeling no emotion. In fact, the people who had the greatest and most beautiful sabr, showed emotion.

Take the example of Prophet Yaqoob (AS) who was severely tested with the loss of his son, Yusuf (AS) and later, Binyamin. He was praised in the Quran for his "Sabrun Jameel" (beautiful patience). And yet Yaqoob (AS) cried until he went blind. Therefore, we know that shedding tears does *not* contradict sabr.

When his son was dying, the Prophet (pbuh) cried. Anas bin Malik narrated:

"The Prophet (pbuh) took Ibrahim and kissed him and smelled him and later we entered Abu Saif's house and at that time Ibrahim was in his last breaths, and the eyes of the Prophet (pbuh) started shedding tears. Abdur Rahman bin `Auf said, 'O Allah's Apostle, even you are weeping!' The Prophet (pbuh) said, "Oh Ibn `Auf, this is mercy." Then he (pbuh) wept more and said, 'The eyes are shedding tears and the heart is grieved, and we will not say anything except what pleases our Lord. O Ibrahim! Indeed we are grieved by your separation.'" (Sahih al-Bukhari 1303)

The idea that emotion and crying are signs of weakness is absolutely false. It is not a weakness, nor it is an oversight in God's design. It is a mercy. Therefore, to deny this natural part of healing is very harmful. If we deny our tears, we stall the healing process. We get in the way of our own healing. This is the divine design of Allah. He gave us tears as a mercy and a cleanse. It is part of the healing process.

Muhammad (pbuh) went through the year of sadness when he lost his wife and his uncle. The Prophets and the righteous companions had emotions and they expressed those emotions. The nickname of Abu Bakr (RA), one of the companions who was promised Paradise, was "al-Baka'a" (the one who cries a lot). In fact, when the Prophet (pbuh) was on his deathbed, he wanted Abu Bakr (RA) to lead the prayer, but Ayesha (RA) was concerned about his excessive crying:

"When the Prophet (pbuh) became ill with his fatal illness, someone came to inform him about the prayer, and the Prophet (pbuh) told him to tell Abu Bakr to lead the people in the prayer. I said, 'Abu Bakr is a soft-hearted man and if he stands for the prayer in your place, he would weep and would not be able to recite the Qur'an.' The Prophet said, 'Tell Abu Bakr to lead the prayer.' I said the same as before. He (repeated the same order and) on the third or the fourth time he said, 'You are the companions of Joseph. Tell Abu Bakr to lead the prayer.'" (Sahih Bukhari, 680)

Even Umar (RA), known for his strength, had marks on his face from tears. There is no contradiction between masculinity and crying, and there is no contradiction between sabr and shedding tears. To see the broken heart, to face it, to feel it, and to acknowledge the pain, takes incredible courage. It takes incredible strength and trust. *Knowing that no matter how broken we feel, no matter how scared we are, that Allah will hold us up and hold us together.* And that He will carry us through. *To truly believe that there is no wound too deep and no pain too great, for Him to heal.* This is what Prophets did.

The Myth of Sabr as Staying in Abuse

The Prophet (pbuh) said:

حَدَّثَنَا مُسَدَّدٌ حَدَّثَنَا مُعْتَمِرٌ عَنْ حُمَيْدٍ عَنْ أَنَسٍ ـ رضى الله عنه ـ قَالَ قَالَ رَسُولُ اللَّهِ صلى الله عليه وسلم انْصُرْ أَخَاكَ ظَالِمًا أَوْ مَظْلُومًا قَالُوا يَا رَسُولَ اللَّهِ هَذَا نَنْصُرُهُ مَظْلُومًا فَكَيْفَ نَنْصُرُهُ ظَالِمًا قَالَ تَأْخُذُ فَوْقَ يَدَيْهِ

"'Help your brother, whether he is an oppressor or he is an oppressed one.' People asked, 'O Allah's Messenger (pbuh)! It is all right to help him if he is oppressed, but how should we help him if he is an oppressor?' The Prophet (pbuh) said, 'By preventing him from oppressing others.'" (Sahih al-Bukhari 2444)

Sometimes we believe that we are being "sacrificial" and "unselfish" by continuing to put up with abuse "for the sake of the children". We think we are helping the abusive person or helping the situation. But the Prophet (pbuh) is teaching us the opposite. He (pbuh) is teaching us that we truly help an oppressor by *stopping him from oppressing*–not by enabling the oppression and "turning the other cheek", then calling it "sabr". Also, our children are an amanah (trust) from Allah, and we will be asked by Allah what we did to protect them. Many people stay in abusive homes "for the sake of the children". But all the evidence shows that children suffer more when they grow up in an abusive home, than if the parents separate. Sadly, these children grow up with many mental health problems due to the trauma of their home life. And many of them end up resenting the parent for staying with the abuser. Some of these children grow up and even leave Islam because of the abusive home. I was told about one child who grew up and left Islam because he said, "I saw my mother praying all the time and reading Quran, but she was absolutely miserable."

Children do not grow up healthy just because their parents stayed under one roof. Children grow up healthy when the home is healthy. Even if that home has a single parent. And even if that means having two homes. Children become healthy when they see their parents healthy and happy. To watch a parent stay miserable or abused, is the worst trauma for a child. To watch a parent put up with infidelity is to teach the child that they should also put up with disrespect in their own marriages. Our children are learning from our choices how to live their own lives. I have seen so many women put up with cheating husbands or abusive husbands because they saw their mother do this. We need to break this cycle of oppression for ourselves and our children. We need to stop misusing religion to condone oppression. If we don't break this cycle, the cycle continues, and we become part of its continuation to the next generation.

Remember that God made divorce halal (permissible) for a reason. It is because sometimes it is the best option. If divorce was always bad, it would have been made haram (forbidden). Any action that is *always bad* is made haram. Alcohol is always bad, so it is haram. Gambling is always bad, so it is haram. Adultery is always bad, so it is haram.

Even the oft-mentioned hadith, "*Divorce is the most hated of the halal*" is in fact classified as a weak *sanad* (chain of narrators). And yet it is constantly repeated, even in situations where it would be *harmful* to stay. The Quran itself speaks about divorce in a very different way than the cultural narrative:

Allah says:

$$\text{الطَّلَاقُ مَرَّتَانِ ۖ فَإِمْسَاكٌ بِمَعْرُوفٍ أَوْ تَسْرِيحٌ بِإِحْسَانٍ ۗ وَلَا}$$

$$\text{يَحِلُّ لَكُمْ أَنْ تَأْخُذُوا مِمَّا آتَيْتُمُوهُنَّ شَيْئًا إِلَّا أَنْ يَخَافَا}$$

$$\text{أَلَّا يُقِيمَا حُدُودَ اللَّهِ ۖ فَإِنْ خِفْتُمْ أَلَّا يُقِيمَا حُدُودَ اللَّهِ}$$

$$\text{فَلَا جُنَاحَ عَلَيْهِمَا فِيمَا افْتَدَتْ بِهِ ۗ تِلْكَ حُدُودُ اللَّهِ فَلَا}$$

$$\text{تَعْتَدُوهَا ۚ وَمَنْ يَتَعَدَّ حُدُودَ اللَّهِ فَأُولَٰئِكَ هُمُ الظَّالِمُونَ ﴿٢٢٩﴾}$$

*"Divorce (may be retracted) twice, then the husband must retain (his wife) with honor or separate (from her) with grace. It is not lawful for husbands to take back anything of the dowry given to their wives, unless the couple fears not being able to keep within the limits of Allah. So if you fear they will not be able to keep within the limits of Allah, **there is no blame** if the wife compensates the husband to obtain divorce (khula). These are the limits set by Allah, so do not transgress them. And whoever transgresses the limits of Allah, they are the 'true' wrongdoers." (Quran 2: 229)*

Allah says "there is no blame" on her if she divorces. Society says there is all the blame on her–even in abuse. And this ayah refers to cases of *khula* (wife-initiated divorce), **where there is no blame on the husband and no harm coming from him.** Allah says there is "no blame" on the wife if she chooses to divorce–even when there is no abuse (khula); what would be the case if there *was* harm coming from him?

The Myth of Sabr as Passive

We are often told that being "patient" means staying still, while burning in the flames. So we practice being passive in abuse, in toxic environments, and poisonous relationships. And then we think ourselves 'patient' and 'righteous'.

The Prophet (pbuh) taught us the exact opposite. He said:

عَنْ أَبِى سَعِيدٍ الْخُدْرِىّ رَضِىَ اللهُ عَنْهُ قَالَ سَمِعْت رَسُولَ
اللَّهِ صلى الله عليه و سلم يَقُولُ مَنْ رَأَى مِنْكُمْ مُنْكَرًا
فَلْيُغَيِّرْهُ بِيَدِهِ فَإِنْ لَمْ يَسْتَطِعْ فَبِلِسَانِهِ فَإِنْ لَمْ يَسْتَطِعْ
فَبِقَلْبِهِ وَذَلِكَ أَضْعَفُ الْإِيمَانِ

رَوَاهُ مُسْلِمٌ

*"Whosoever of you sees an evil, let him change it with his hand; and if he
is not able to do so, then [let him change it] with his tongue; and if he is
not able to do so, then with his heart — and that is the weakest of faith."*
(Sahih Muslim 49)

The Prophet (pbuh) is not defining righteousness as being passive. In
fact, he says the opposite. He is teaching us that there is a link between faith
(iman) and *taking action* against oppression, because the weakest of iman is
at least hating oppression in our hearts.

Despite this fact, some people sit passively, waiting to be saved. And
many people believe this is the meaning of sabr. But, what did Hajar do
when her husband, Ibrahim (AS), had to leave her in the desert alone with
baby Ismael (AS)? When she found herself stranded, did she lay down and
wait for water to fall from the skies? Did she *sit* and wait to be saved?

No. She *ran.*

She *strove.* She did what every Muslim must now do to complete pil-
grimage: she did 'Sa'ee' (to strive). She ran between Safaa and Marwa. And
not once. Or twice. She didn't give up and she didn't lose hope, although
each time she found only empty hilltops. She kept going. She kept striving.
She kept hoping. And only after seven times of her **striving** was she saved
by God, and water miraculously came from the sand.

I remember a point in my own life when I felt totally defeated. And in
that moment, I felt like giving up. On everything. *Everything.*

It made me wonder what Hajar (AS) felt each time she reached a hilltop, only to find nothing. Again, nothing. Just another false hope. But, I suppose no hope is ever really false. Yet, I wondered sometimes how she found the will to keep going. How she found the strength to get back up each time. Get up, and run again…when maybe all she wanted to do was quit.

I guess I've lived through a lot of empty hilltops. *A lot.* I've stopped at some and cried. Sometimes I've knelt. Sometimes I've fallen to my knees. But that's exactly it. It isn't the ups and downs that define us. It's what we do *after*. It's how we keep going. It wasn't the empty hilltop that defined Hajar's journey. It wasn't the one, or three, or even six 'false hopes'. It was her telling herself and God, seven painful times, that she isn't perfect, and neither is this life. And that it's full of disappointments and mirages and illusions. That things are going to hurt. That we're going to be thirsty–dying of thirst in a desert sometimes. And sometimes we're going to find nothing. Again and again and again, find nothing.

And then we may begin to wonder, if maybe the problem is *me*. Maybe *I'm* the problem. Maybe there's something broken in me or maybe just something weak. And maybe there is. Maybe we're not perfect. Maybe we're *full of flaws*. But, dear God, we are still running. We are still going. We get back up. We get back up because even a person who can't move can still pray with the eyes.

And even a person who can't speak, can still scream out with the heart.
And to the All-Hearing, the silent screams are loud.

True Meaning of Sabr and its Reward

SABR: THE GREATEST PROVISION

It's important to understand that sabr itself is a gift from God. It is not an inherent quality in any human being. In fact, part of our human nature is the inclination towards *imp*atience. Only those who strive against this lower inclination will be given the gift of Sabr. And if we are given this gift, it is the most comprehensive gift we can be given.

The Messenger of Allah (pbuh) said:

"Whoever strives to be patient, then Allah will make him patient. And there is no gift that is better and more comprehensive than patience." (Sahīh al-Bukhārī 1469)

وَمَنْ يَتَصَبَّرْ يُصَبِّرْهُ اللَّه

وَمَا أُعْطِيَ أَحَدٌ عَطَاءً

خَيْرًا وَأَوْسَعَ مِنْ الصَّبْرِ

ELEVATION AND PURIFICATION OF SABR

There will be times in life, where we cannot change the circumstances of a test, such as the death of a loved one, or incurable disease or disability. In these cases, showing sabr (patience) means acceptance. And by showing sabr through these trials, we are elevated and purified.

We may also become elevated through the test of relational injury. Sometimes other people become the "sandpaper" by which we are polished and purified. It is important to reiterate here that this does not mean we are passive about abuse or mistreatment. We are commanded to take action against injustice and oppression. But there will be times when, despite all our efforts, we are still hurt or oppressed at the hands of others. And the oppressor can be the means by which we are polished. Through the trial itself, we are given the gift of sabr. And through that gift, we may also have our sins forgiven because of the painful loss or (unavoidable) injustice we experienced.

The Prophet (pbuh) said:

"No fatigue, nor disease, nor sorrow, nor sadness, nor hurt, nor distress befalls a Muslim, even if it were the prick of a thorn, but that Allah expiates some of his sins for that." (Sahih Bukhari 5641, 5642)

مَا يُصِيبُ الْمُسْلِمَ مِنْ

نَصَبٍ وَلاَ وَصَبٍ وَلاَ هَمٍّ

وَلاَ حُزْنٍ وَلاَ أَذًى وَلاَ غَمٍّ

حَتَّى الشَّوْكَةِ يُشَاكُهَا إِلاَّ

كَفَّرَ اللَّهُ بِهَا مِنْ خَطَايَاهُ

Allah says:

*Say, "O My servants who have
believed, have consciousness of
your Lord. For those who do good
in this world is goodness, and the
earth of Allah is spacious. Indeed,
those who endure patiently shall
receive their reward without
limit." (Quran 39:10)*

قُلْ يَا عِبَادِ الَّذِينَ آمَنُوا
اتَّقُوا رَبَّكُمْ لِلَّذِينَ
أَحْسَنُوا فِي هَذِهِ الدُّنْيَا
حَسَنَةٌ وَأَرْضُ اللَّهِ وَاسِعَةٌ
إِنَّمَا يُوَفَّى الصَّابِرُونَ
أَجْرَهُمْ بِغَيْرِ حِسَابٍ ﴿١٠﴾

This ayah is so powerful. It teaches us that when we do good, we *get
good*—in this life and the next. And that the reward of sabr is unlike anything
else, as Allah says its reward is without limit.

The Quran also tells us that the reward of patience is high places in
paradise, with greetings of peace:

*"Those are the ones who will be
rewarded with the highest place
in heaven, because of their patient
constancy: therein they shall be
met with salutations and peace."
(Quran 25:75)*

أُولَئِكَ يُجْزَوْنَ الْغُرْفَةَ بِمَا
صَبَرُوا وَيُلَقَّوْنَ فِيهَا تَحِيَّةً
وَسَلَامًا ﴿٧٥﴾

TRIALS, SABR AND LEADERSHIP

After Sabr and Certainty

We are also told in the Quran that the process of elevation in true leadership only comes after trials that are followed by Sabr:

"And We made from among them leaders, guiding (others) by Our command when they were patient and [when] they were certain of Our signs."(Quran 32:24)

وَجَعَلْنَا مِنْهُمْ أَئِمَّةً يَهْدُونَ بِأَمْرِنَا لَمَّا صَبَرُوا ۖ وَكَانُوا بِآيَاتِنَا يُوقِنُونَ ﴿٢٤﴾

In this ayah, Allah tells us that true leadership may be granted after two things happen: A person is tested and shows patience and that person becomes certain of Allah's signs (yaqeen).

After Sabr in Obedience

In another ayah, Allah teaches us that true leadership is given after obedience to His commands, even when it involves sacrifice:

And [mention, O Muhammad], when Abraham was tried by his Lord with commands and he fulfilled them. [Allah] said, "Indeed, I will make you a leader for the people." [Abraham] said, "And of my descendants?" [Allah] said, "My covenant does not include the wrongdoers." (Quran 2:124)

وَإِذِ ابْتَلَىٰ إِبْرَاهِيمَ رَبُّهُ بِكَلِمَاتٍ فَأَتَمَّهُنَّ ۖ قَالَ إِنِّي جَاعِلُكَ لِلنَّاسِ إِمَامًا ۖ قَالَ وَمِن ذُرِّيَّتِي ۖ قَالَ لَا يَنَالُ عَهْدِي الظَّالِمِينَ ﴿١٢٤﴾

SABR AND SUCCESS

Allah says:

*"O you who have believed,
persevere, and endure and remain
stationed and have consciousness of
God, that you may be successful."*
(Quran 3:200)

يَا أَيُّهَا الَّذِينَ آمَنُوا اصْبِرُوا
وَصَابِرُوا وَرَابِطُوا وَاتَّقُوا
اللَّهَ لَعَلَّكُمْ تُفْلِحُونَ ﴿٢٠٠﴾

In this ayah, Allah is addressing the believers and providing a formula for *Ultimate Success*. The formula has 4 parts:

اصْبِرُوا-Have Sabr

صَابِرُوا- Exceed others in Sabr and against your own evil inclinations

رَابِطُوا-Stand firm, stationed and ready

وَاتَّقُوا-Have God Consciousness

When you examine these four parts, you realize that 3 out of 4 parts of the formula for success involve a form of Sabr.

SABR LOOKS DIFFERENT DEPENDING ON THE SITUATION

Sabr will take different forms depending on the situation. When Allah has commanded something, sabr means persevering in carrying out that action. When Allah has forbidden something, sabr means restraining yourself against it. When Allah has decreed something and we cannot change it, sabr means acceptance without resentment.

Sabr in His commands

When Allah gives a command, sabr means obedience. For example, Allah has commanded us to pray 5 times a day, at specified times. Sabr in this case is our *perseverance* to maintain all of our prayers and on time. Allah has also commanded us to take action against injustice and abuse. So in this case, sabr would be our fight to free ourselves and others from oppression. Sabr is not passive. Sabr was required for the companions who were fighting in battle, just as much as it is required for us while fighting the battles of our life…our own battles against injustice.

Sabr against His prohibitions

When Allah has prohibited something, sabr means restraining ourselves from that which has been prohibited. For example, Allah has prohibited us from looking at the haram. Sabr is required for us to consistently lower our gaze. Allah has also prohibited food, water and intimacy during the daytime in Ramadan. Sabr is required to restrain ourselves while fasting.

Sabr in His uncontrollable decrees

When there is nothing we can do to change a situation—such as a death or disability—sabr means acceptance. It means restraining the self from complaining "against" Allah and His decree. We can complain *to* Allah, but not *against* Allah.

COMPLAINING TO ALLAH VS. COMPLAINING ABOUT ALLAH

Prophet Yaqoob (AS) turned to Allah in his pain. He complained *to* Allah:

"He said, 'I only complain of my suffering and my grief to Allah, and I know from Allah that which you do not know.'" (Quran 12:86)

قَالَ إِنَّمَا أَشْكُو بَثِّي وَحُزْنِي إِلَى اللَّهِ وَأَعْلَمُ مِنَ اللَّهِ مَا لَا تَعْلَمُونَ ﴿٨٦﴾

There is a vital difference between complaining *about* Allah and complaining *to* Allah. Complaining *about* Allah is to show anger and resentment towards God and His decree. Complaining *to* Allah is what the Prophets did. They turned to Allah in humility and brokenness and begged for help. They put their trust in Allah; they never relied on themselves.

During the year of sadness, after losing his wife and uncle, the Prophet (pbuh) traveled to Taif to seek support from its people. Instead of giving him support, the people of Taif abused the Prophet (pbuh) and violently pushed him out of the city. Many years later, the Prophet (pbuh) told his wife Ayesha (RA), that this experience was the hardest point of his life. In the midst of the most difficult moment of his life, after all he had just experienced, Muhammad (pbuh) turned to Allah and called out with this duaa:

اللّهُمَّ إِلَيْكَ أَشْكُو ضَعْفَ قُوَّتِي ، وَقِلَّةَ حِيلَتِي ، وَهَوَانِي عَلَى النَّاسِ، يَا أَرْحَمَ الرّاحِمِينَ ! أَنْتَ رَبّ الْمُسْتَضْعَفِينَ وَأَنْتَ رَبِّي ، إِلَى مَنْ تَكِلُنِي ؟ إِلَى بَعِيدٍ يَتَجَهَّمُنِي ؟ أَمْ إِلَى عَدُوٍّ مَلَّكْتَهُ أَمْرِي ؟ إِنْ لَمْ يَكُنْ بِكَ عَلَيَّ غَضَبٌ فَلَا أُبَالِي ، وَلَكِنَّ عَافِيَتَكَ هِيَ أَوْسَعُ لِي ، أَعُوذُ بِنُورِ وَجْهِكَ الَّذِي أَشْرَقَتْ لَهُ الظُّلُمَاتُ وَصَلُحَ عَلَيْهِ أَمْرُ الدَّنْيَا وَالْآخِرَةِ مِنْ أَنْ تُنْزِلَ بِي غَضَبَكَ ، أَوْ يَحِلَّ عَلَيَّ سُخْطَكَ، لَكَ الْعُتْبَى حَتّى تَرْضَى ، وَلَا حَوْلَ وَلَا قُوَّةَ إِلَّا بِكَ

"To You, my Lord, I complain of my weakness, lack of support and the humiliation I receive (from people). Most Compassionate and Merciful! You are the Lord of the weak, and you are my Lord. To whom do You leave me? To a distant person who receives me with hostility? Or to an enemy You have given power over me? As long as you are not displeased with me, I do not care what I face. However, Your 'Aafiyah' (well-being, safety) is more expansive for me. I seek refuge in the Light of Your face—which illuminates the heavens and earth, and by which all darkness is dispelled, and all matters of this life and the next are set right—against incurring Your wrath or being the subject to Your anger. To You I submit, until I earn Your pleasure. Everything is powerless without Your support." (al Tabarani)

In this powerful duaa, the Prophet (pbuh) is complaining *to* Allah, but not *about* Allah. He is turning to Allah for help, in humility and need. His complaint is against himself and his own "human weakness". And he is seeking refuge in Allah and His light. The Prophet (pbuh) is also setting the focus of his heart on what matters most: the pleasure of Allah in any given situation. He says, "If you are not displeased with me, I do not mind." Despite this, the Prophet (pbuh) is also asking for ease when he says: "However, Your 'Aafiyah' (well-being, safety) is more expansive for me."

Ask Allah for Aafiyah, Not Sabr

In the duaa of Taif, the Prophet (pbuh) is asking Allah for عَافِيَتُكَ (God's Aafiyah), not sabr. This is an important concept. Aafiyah is a comprehensive term that includes well-being, ease and safety from calamity and difficulty. He has advised us not to ask for sabr, but to ask for Aafiyah instead:

The Prophet (pbuh) heard a man saying: "Oh Allah, I ask You for patience (sabr)." The Prophet (pbuh) said: "You have asked Allah for calamity; rather ask Him for well-being (Aafiyah)." (at-Tirmidhi 3527)

We know the immense reward of sabr during calamities, but we should never ask for calamities. Instead, we should ask for ease and safety from calamities (Aafiyah). If we are faced with trials, we should show sabr, but ask for ease and relief.

Barrier 2:
Negative Thinking

When we indulge, entertain, and feed negative thoughts, we sabotage our own healing and happiness. Thoughts will always "knock on the door of our minds." Our thoughts are like visitors that knock at our home. Imagine that someone is knocking on your door and when you look through the peephole, you see that it is your neighbor, carrying food and flowers. In this case, you are likely to open the door and let them in. You will invite them to sit down and perhaps offer something to eat or drink.

But what happens if you hear a knock and when you look through the peephole, you see a man holding a machine gun, a knife, and a grenade? Would you open the door, in that case? Would you invite the man in and offer him tea and cookies? Would you ask him to stay? Definitely not. But unfortunately, this is exactly what we do when our negative thoughts "knock" on the door of our mind. Our negative thoughts are like that man standing at our door, holding weapons. He is there to do harm. He is not there to give us flowers or food or glad tidings. He is there to destroy us and the sanctuary of our home. And yet, many of us give him free access. When we have a negative thought and it is knocking on the door of our mind, we often open the door to that thought. We feed it. We let it stay the night.

Negative Thoughts About Others

For example, when the negative thought is about another person, what do we often do? Do we keep the thought out by having *husnul dhan* (positive assumptions/giving the benefit of the doubt)? Or do we allow the thought to come in and do we feed it? What happens when you feed something? It grows. And it can become a monster inside our minds. Often we indulge and entertain destructive thoughts. We give them space and time in our mind and heart.

Toxic Self-Talk

Another type of negative thought that can "knock" on the door of your mind, is toxic self-talk. Having a negative self-concept (negative image of oneself) will prolong the healing process. For example, if someone leaves or breaks up with you, a person with a negative self-concept might attribute it to being "unlovable", "not attractive enough", or "unworthy". These negative cognitions sabotage your own healing and lead to toxic self-talk. If negative self-talk knocks on the door of your mind and tells you that you are not good enough, do you allow it in? Do you give those thoughts space and fuel, or do you keep the door shut? We know that our words with others can build–or destroy. But, do we realize that our words with ourselves can do the same? *Toxic self-talk is one of the most destructive psychological and spiritual forces.*

We must view our thoughts and inner dialogue like we view a visitor that comes to our door. Think of how diligently we guard our homes and valuables. We use locks, security systems, and fences. We do not open the door for just anyone. And if a robber shows up at our front door carrying weapons, we would never willingly open the door to him. No one would invite him in, feed him food, give him tea, and ask him to stay the night. And yet, this is exactly what we do with negative thoughts that knock on the door of our minds and hearts. We cannot control *who* knocks on our door (of home or mind). But we *can* control who we *let in*. Who we feed. And who we invite to stay the night.

Just as our home is a well-guarded sanctuary, so should our mind and heart be. We cannot allow destructive thoughts to enter and live in this sanctuary. If we do, these destructive thoughts and negative self-dialogue will cause serious damage. Negative self-talk is poisonous. When we think negatively, when we beat ourselves up, when we lack self-compassion, we are actually drinking poison. We must be mindful of our thoughts and how we speak to ourselves. If our self-talk is self-deprecating, we must stop and replace it with more healthy talk, compassionate speech. Replace thoughts like, "I'm such a failure" with thoughts like, "I'm doing my best and I can try again." When we speak to ourselves, we should ask, "Is this the way I would speak to a loved one?" We know that if we did speak to a friend or spouse or boss in the same negative way we sometimes speak to ourselves, we would destroy that relationship. Unfortunately, many of us are destroying our relationships with ourselves.

Living in the Past

Sometimes the negative mind visitor is something from our past. Sadly, many of us keep our wounds fresh by living in the past, unable to move forward. There are several factors that can keep us chained to the past, such as regret, trauma or mental illness. When we are paralyzed by regret over a sin or by a past mistake/poor decision, we cannot fully move forward.

REGRET OVER SIN

If our regret is over a sin, we should not fixate on the sin, but rather go through the process of sincere repentance and then move on with full hope that we have been forgiven. *Our focus should not be on the greatness of the sin, but rather on the greatness of Allah's forgiveness.* Allah has promised us in the Quran that when we sincerely repent for a sin, not only is that sin erased from our Record, the sin is transformed into a good deed.

Allah says:

"Except for those who repent, believe and do righteous work. For them Allah will replace their evil deeds with good. And ever is Allah Forgiving and Merciful." (Quran 25:70)

إِلَّا مَنْ تَابَ وَآمَنَ وَعَمِلَ عَمَلًا صَالِحًا فَأُولَٰئِكَ يُبَدِّلُ اللَّهُ سَيِّئَاتِهِمْ حَسَنَاتٍ وَكَانَ اللَّهُ غَفُورًا رَحِيمًا ٧٠

REGRET OVER NEGATIVE OUTCOMES

If the regret is due to a negative outcome due to what we perceive as a poor decision, we must take the lessons from our past, but we cannot get stuck there. We cannot live there. As Roy T. Bennet wrote: "*The past is a place of reference, not a place of residence; the past is a place of learning, not a place of living.*" When a person gets stuck in the pain or illusions of their past, it becomes a barrier to healing and progress. Some people relive or replay parts of their past and it becomes a deterrent from moving forward.

The Prophet (pbuh) said:

"...If anything befalls you, do not say, 'if only I had done such and such' rather say 'Qaddara Allahu wa ma sha'a fa'ala (Allah has decreed and whatever He wills, He does).' For (saying) "If" opens (the door) to the deeds of Satan."' (Sahih, Sunan Ibn Majah 79)

TRAUMA OR MENTAL ILLNESS

There are times when reliving the past is due to unhealed trauma (PTSD) and may require therapy to heal and move forward. There is no shame in seeking help to heal from a painful past. In fact, seeking help can be rewardable as an act of worship (*ibaadah*). Sometimes painful, intrusive thoughts can be due to mental illness such as Obsessive Compulsive Disorder (OCD). When obsessive thoughts become so overwhelming that they interfere with normal functioning (such as taking 30 minutes to make wudu or obsessively thinking about death, etc.), this can be a sign of OCD and requires therapy to heal. Every person on this earth is tested in different ways. For some people, poverty is their test. For other people, sickness is their test. And for some people, mental illness is their test. Allah decides who and how He appoints His soldiers for different internal and external battles. And it is Allah who also showers His mercy and His assistance and reward upon those He tests.

Anxiety

Another negative thought that can knock on the door of our mind is fear. When it is fear that knocks on the door of our mind, what happens? At first, the fear may be tiny. But what happens when we let it in and feed it?

What happens when we imagine, and mentally live out, all the worst possible outcomes that could happen? What happens when we play out every scenario of these horrible things in our mind? What does that do to our level of fear and anxiety? What does that do to our body? All these terrible "what if" scenarios actually trigger the stress response and push our bodies into "fight-or-flight mode". Through our thoughts, we are literally experiencing the terrible outcome as if it had already happened. So our heart rate increases, our breathing changes, and our blood sugar and blood pressure shoot up. Our body is reacting to our thoughts, but nothing has actually happened.

HEALTHY WAY TO DEAL WITH FEARS

It is natural to have fears. It is natural to be afraid of certain outcomes. But, is there a healthier way to deal with our fears? What should you do if fear or doubt knocks on your door?

Step 1: Make duaa

Do not open the door for the fear, but make duaa about what you are afraid of. Keep your heart and mind protected by keeping the door shut, but focus on duaa for protection. If you are afraid of a certain outcome, ask Allah to prevent or protect you or your family from that outcome. Sometimes, a fear knocks on our heart to inspire that duaa, and because of that duaa, we are protected from the harm. The fear inspired the duaa, and the duaa became the means of protection from Allah.

Step 2: Take action

Ask yourself, "Is there an action that I can or should take to protect myself or others from the fear that I have?" If the answer is "yes", and that action is permissible (halal) and legal and healthy, then take that action.

After both steps 1 and 2 have been taken, do not entertain that fear anymore. Its time and space on your doorstep has expired. Do not open the door. Do not let it in or feed it. The next time it knocks again, just repeat steps 1 and 2. And then let it go and keep the door shut.

THE USE OF FEAR

Shaytan tries to use fear as a weapon against us. He tries to keep us locked up inside of fear and despair. Fear becomes a chain that paralyzes us and prevents us from living fulfilling lives or getting closer to Allah. But, if you continue to repeat these steps (duaa + action), fear transforms from being a weapon of Satan against us, to being a means of getting closer to Allah through duaa and reliance on Him. Every time you are afraid of something, use it to make duaa and seek help from Allah. Therefore, even the fear itself can bring you closer to Allah. And if that fear is coming from waswasa (shaytan's whispers), shaytan will stop putting it in your mind because it will end up bringing you closer to Allah.

Scarcity mindset

Allah tells us in the Quran:

"Satan frightens you with poverty and orders you to immorality, while Allah promises you forgiveness from Him and bounty. And Allah is all-Encompassing and Knowing." (Quran 2:268)

الشَّيْطَانُ يَعِدُكُمُ الْفَقْرَ
وَيَأْمُرُكُم بِالْفَحْشَاءِ وَاللَّهُ
يَعِدُكُم مَّغْفِرَةً مِّنْهُ وَفَضْلًا
وَاللَّهُ وَاسِعٌ عَلِيمٌ ﴿٢٦٨﴾

Shaytan uses fear and a *scarcity mentality* to keep us paralyzed. A scarcity mindset is when you are so obsessed with the *lack* of something, that you cannot focus on anything else. With a scarcity mindset, your thoughts and actions stem from a place of fear. It's an obsession with what's missing and the fear of loss. It's a focus on your *poverty*, rather than your *richness*. It keeps you scared, and it robs you of your power. A *scarcity* or *survival mentality* affects the brain and even causes it to function differently. Because the brain believes there is a threat of some sort (not enough, fear of loss), it triggers a stress response. Specifically, a scarcity mindset obstructs two things: rationality and generosity.

Cannot act rationally or problem solve

The stress response does not allow a person to act rationally. When a person is in fight-or-flight mode, they do not use their frontal cortex, but instead use the "old brain" because they are simply in survival mode. When we are not using our higher reasoning, we will make poor choices. These poor choices end up being ultimately self-sabotaging, as we are not able to think and decide rationally, taking into account the "big picture". The fight or flight mode makes an individual have "tunnel vision". In other words, the individual becomes fixated on that one fear, such that they do not see what is around it. As a result, they make imbalanced decisions. One can never attain balance if they are being driven by fear. It actually limits your brain function. Scarcity mentality affects your ability to solve problems, hold information, and reason logically. It also affects your brain's decision-making process. A scarcity mindset limits your ability to plan, focus, and start a project or task. Your brain is too busy thinking about something you don't have. In fact, having a scarcity mentality can lower your IQ by as many as 14 points. If you have an average IQ, losing 13 or 14 points can make it fall into the deficient category.

Psychologist Daniel Goleman called the overreaction to stress "amygdala hijack" in his 1995 book, *"Emotional Intelligence: Why It Can Matter More Than IQ."* In stressful situations, the amygdala (emotional brain) hijacks control of your response. The amygdala disables the frontal lobes and activates the fight-or-flight response. Without the frontal lobes, you can't think clearly, make rational decisions, or control your responses. Control has been "hijacked" by the amygdala.

When faced with a "threatening situation", the thalamus sends sensory information to both the amygdala and the neocortex. If the amygdala senses danger, it makes a split-second decision to initiate the fight-or-flight response, before the neocortex has time to overrule it.

This cascade of events triggers the release of stress hormones, including the hormones epinephrine (also known as adrenaline) and cortisol. Cortisol (the stress hormone) suppresses immunity and digestion, and increases blood pressure, heart rate, and blood sugar. Temporarily, the stress response is adaptive. But a chronic stress response leads to many illnesses, such as diabetes, heart disease, ulcers, and even cancer.

Cannot act generously

Secondly, when a person is in survival mode, they cannot act generously. They will instinctively become stingy and self-serving. An extreme example of this response is illustrated in the Quran regarding the Day of Judgment. We are told that due to extreme terror, people will be willing to sacrifice their own children, spouse, and loved ones.

Allah says: "They will be made to see each other. The wicked will wish to ransom themselves from the punishment of that Day by their children, their spouses, their siblings, their clan that sheltered them, and everyone on earth altogether, just to save themselves." (Quran 70:11-14)

Allah also says: "But when there comes the Deafening Blast. On the Day a man will flee from his brother. And his mother and his father. And his wife and his children. For every man, that Day, will be an adequate matter for him." (Quran 80: 33-37)

Take for example a less extreme scenario. In Ramadan at large iftars, what happens to the behavior of people when they believe there is a shortage of food? Even the most polite of people will begin to act selfishly. People may skip the line and hoard food. We saw the same phenomenon during the Covid-19 lockdown. Normally at the grocery store, people buy just enough for what they need to feed their families. But, when people started to fear scarcity, they acted out of that fear and began to hoard selfishly. Even Black Friday sales can become violent due to this fear of "not enough", fear of missing out, "poverty".

In a profound hadith, the Prophet (pbuh) explains that one of the root causes of this mindset is hyperfocus on dunya–rather than akhira (hereafter):

مَنْ كَانَتْ الْآخِرَةُ هَمَّهُ جَعَلَ اللَّهُ غِنَاهُ فِي قَلْبِهِ وَجَمَعَ لَهُ شَمْلَهُ وَأَتَتْهُ الدُّنْيَا وَهِيَ رَاغِمَةٌ وَمَنْ كَانَتْ الدُّنْيَا هَمَّهُ جَعَلَ اللَّهُ فَقْرَهُ بَيْنَ عَيْنَيْهِ وَفَرَّقَ عَلَيْهِ شَمْلَهُ وَلَمْ يَأْتِهِ مِنْ الدُّنْيَا إِلَّا مَا قُدِّرَ لَهُ

*"Whoever makes the Hereafter his **primary** concern, Allah will place contentment in his heart, will make his affairs come together, and the world will come to him, even if it is reluctant to do so. Whoever makes this life his **primary** concern, Allah will place his poverty between his eyes, will scatter his affairs, and he will not get anything from this world, except what has been decreed for him."* (Sunan al-Tirmidhī 2465)

The Prophet (pbuh) is teaching us that one of the consequences of making this life our primary concern, is that "poverty is put between our eyes". What happens if something is stuck between our eyes? Can we ever escape seeing it? No matter which direction we look, we see whatever is stuck there. So in this case, no matter where we look, we would always "see" poverty. In other words, no matter what the person has, he will always feel that it's not enough.

He will always feel "poor". And if someone feels poor, he will not be able to act generously. Instead, he will always be coveting *more* for himself, rather than giving to others.

Consumed by fear

By using this formula, Shaytan successfully employs fear to make us act indecent and stingy, in order to save ourselves from what we fear (poverty, loss, etc.). But the first step in acting indecent or stingy is to become *consumed by fear*. Once we are consumed by fear, we become a prisoner to it. And we will begin to act in ways that go against our morals and principles. When someone is desperate, they are more willing to break the rules of God and society. Hence, Shaytan uses fear as a weapon to make human beings act immorally.

Barrier 3:
Shame

Shame vs. Healthy Remorse/Guilt

Another factor that delays healing is shame. We learn from Quran 2:268 that after using fear to put us into a scarcity mentality, Shaytan calls us to indecency and immorality to "save ourselves" from what we fear. When we are afraid and enter "survival mode", we are more likely to act against our own morals and principles, in this desperate attempt to "save ourselves". And the more intense the fear–the more desperate we feel–the more willing we will be to cross boundaries to protect ourselves. The more fixated we are on the "end", the more likely we are to convince ourselves that any means justify that end. And so we act indecently. Then once we act indecently, we are likely to enter into *shame*.

Once we are in shame, we often fall into despair. We may believe we are not worthy of Allah's love and mercy and forgiveness. And then we give up on trying to attain Allah's pleasure and nearness, ultimately because we feel we don't deserve it. And so in ayah 2: 268, Allah contrasts this plot of shaytan, which uses fear and indecency, with Allah's mercy and bounty and abundance. *The antidote for shame is mercy and compassion. The antidote for scarcity/fear of poverty is abundance and God's bounty and grace.*

According to Brené Brown, a researcher at the University of Houston, shame is an "intensely painful feeling or experience of believing that we are flawed and therefore unworthy of love and belonging."

The difference between healthy remorse and shame is that remorse says, "I *did* something bad", while shame says, "I *am* bad". Remorse focuses on a behavior, while shame focuses on the *self.* Remorse makes you concerned about the feelings of others, while shame makes you only concerned with your own feelings of worthlessness. Shame does not motivate change because it leads to hopelessness. If I believe that I *am* bad, I will feel powerless to improve things. Thus, shame is highly correlated with things like addiction, depression, violence, and aggression. Shame will make you want to run away from the problem, while remorse will motivate you to fix it.

Spiritually, shame is very dangerous because it makes you want to hide from Allah, rather than seek forgiveness and try again. That is why shame is an effective tool of Shaytan. Shame leads to more rebellion and immorality because the person believes that they are "bad" and "not worthy". So the person either engages in escape behaviors or the person behaves in ways that are congruent with their negative belief of the self. Hence, Allah says "Satan frightens you with poverty and orders you to immorality, while Allah promises you forgiveness from Him and bounty..." (Quran 2:268) Shame and scarcity lead to further transgression; remorse and hope lead to redemption and repentance.

God's Mercy vs. Man's Shame

One fascinating and effective way to learn about the Creator is to study His creation close up. Take, for example, human beings and how humans respond to others who have made mistakes.

In classic literature, authors often examine this element of human nature and society. For example, Nathaniel Hawthorne wrote about a woman living in Puritan America, in his classic novel, *The Scarlet Letter.* Because the woman had committed adultery, she was forced by society to wear a giant "A" around her neck for the rest of her life. This was intended to shame her by putting her sin on display for all to see.

In contrast to the shaming culture of society, one of the attributes of Allah is Al-Sateer, the One who conceals. Unlike human beings, who can be cruel and unforgiving, Allah not only forgives, He also *conceals* our sins.

Take, for example, the most powerful supplication for repentance. The Prophet (pbuh) said: "Whoever says this duaa as he enters upon evening, then, dies that night, he would **enter Paradise**; and if one says this as he enters upon morning, then, dies that day, he would enter Paradise."

اللّٰهُمَّ أَنْتَ رَبِّي لَا إِلٰهَ إِلَّا أَنْتَ خَلَقْتَنِي وَأَنَا عَبْدُكَ وَأَنَا عَلَى عَهْدِكَ وَوَعْدِكَ مَا اسْتَطَعْتُ أَعُوذُ بِكَ مِنْ شَرِّ مَا صَنَعْتُ أَبُوءُ لَكَ بِنِعْمَتِكَ عَلَيَّ وَأَبُوءُ بِذَنْبِي فَاغْفِرْ لِي فَإِنَّهُ لَا يَغْفِرُ الذُّنُوبَ إِلَّا أَنْتَ

"O Allah, You are my Lord, none has the right to be worshiped except You, You created me and I am Your servant and I abide to Your covenant and promise, as best I can. I seek refuge in You from the evil of which I have committed. I acknowledge Your favor upon me and I acknowledge my sin, so forgive me, for verily none can forgive sin except You." (Sahih al Bukhari 6306)

In the very last part of the duaa, we say: "faghfirli fa innahu la yaghfir athunooba illa ent."

"Forgive me...for verily none can forgive sin, except You."

This is very deep. There are several different words in the Arabic language for "sin" ("ithm", "sayiaat", "ma'siyah", "fahshaa", "mukhar"). But, the specific word used here is "Thunoob". This word comes from the root, which means "tail". In other words, our sins become like tails that follow us around, like a "Scarlet Letter". And people never forget them. Never erase them. Maybe some people may even continuously remind us of them. Allah does not. Allah does not remind us of our sins after repentance. "No one forgives the sins (tail), except You." After repentance, Allah does not judge us by what we regret from our past. Allah does not mention it again. He does not shame us. He erases "the tail" (our sin). And not only does He erase it, He even converts those same sins into good deeds.

Allah says:

"Except for those who repent,
believe and do righteous work.
For them Allah will replace their
evil deeds with good. And ever is
Allah Forgiving and Merciful."
(Quran 25:70)

إِلَّا مَنْ تَابَ وَآمَنَ وَعَمِلَ
عَمَلًا صَالِحًا فَأُولَٰئِكَ يُبَدِّلُ
اللَّهُ سَيِّئَاتِهِمْ حَسَنَاتٍ وَكَانَ
اللَّهُ غَفُورًا رَحِيمًا ﴿٧٠﴾

The same thing which becomes the cause of ridicule from the creation, becomes the cause of honor from the Creator. And, verily, no one forgives sins—except Him. If for nothing else, love Him for that. *While the creation may force you to wear your badge of shame around your neck forever, the Creator honors you after repentance.*

It is reported in Sahih Muslim that a woman came to the Prophet (pbuh) and confessed to committing Adultery; she even requested that her sentence be carried out. At last the Prophet (pbuh) commanded that it was time to carry out the sentence. After her death, the Prophet (pbuh) led her funeral prayers. Omar (RA) questioned, "Oh Messenger of Allah! She committed Zina (adultery) and you have performed funeral prayers for her?" The Prophet (pbuh) replied, "Verily, she made repentance which would suffice for seventy of the people of Al-Madinah if it was divided among them." (Sahih Muslim)

Although this woman had indeed committed adultery, the Prophet (pbuh) did not allow the people to disrespect or verbally abuse her. And he made sure she was honored after her repentance.

Barrier 4: Lack of Self Compassion

Another factor that delays healing is lack of self-compassion and excessive self-blame. When bad things happen, or things don't work out, or we lose something we love, many people internalize all the blame. Believing that it is "all your fault" or that the negative event happened because of you alone, will delay healing.

Growth requires introspection and accountability, but this should be done with compassion and balance. No one is perfectly good; but, no one is perfectly bad either. If we have made mistakes or have elements in us that need to change, we should address these *with mercy*. We should recognize that Allah did not create us perfect and therefore does not expect perfection from us.

We all have flaws. The best of people are not the "flawless". To believe we are flawless is delusional arrogance (ghuroor). The best of people are the ones who recognize their own humanness and hold themselves accountable *with compassion*. They accept that they have imperfections, while also trying to improve and grow. This is the model taught to us by Allah and His messenger (pbuh). The Prophet (pbuh) said:

"All of the children of Adam are bound to make mistakes, and the best of those who make mistakes are those who repent." (Sunan al-Tirmidhī 2499)

كُلُّ ابْنِ آدَمَ خَطَّاءٌ وَخَيْرُ الْخَطَّائِينَ التَّوَّابُونَ

Believing we are, or can be, perfect is a trap of Shaytan. Ironically, it is the cause of both arrogance and despair. If we believe we *are* perfect, that is self-deception (ghuroor) and arrogance (ujb). And if we believe we need to be perfect or sinless, the moment we slip, we will fall into despair. This is what Shaytan wants. He wants us to be arrogant or he wants us to give up. He wants us to think that we are either too good to have to try, or that we are too "bad" and "worthless" to keep trying. He wants us to believe that Islam is "all or none". Before we sin, he tells us that Allah's mercy is so great. Then after we sin, he tells us Allah's mercy isn't great enough. When we slip, he makes us think, "What's the point of wearing hijab or praying or going to the masjid? I'm just being a hypocrite!"

But it was the belief in perfection that was flawed. The arrogance or despair is what follows that flawed assumption. The starting point of perfectionism was wrong; so the result is destructive.

Barrier 5:
Lack of Closure or Acceptance

Another factor that delays healing is not having closure or acceptance of the situation. In his book, *How to Fix A Broken Heart*, psychologist Guy Winch discusses one of his clients who was devastated after the man she expected to marry, broke up with her. Dr. Winch explains how the woman's healing process was delayed excessively because she was unwilling to accept the reason the man gave for the breakup. Instead of accepting the reason he gave on face value, she decided that there must have been another "hidden reason". She spent the next 12 months trying to figure out what that "real" reason was. The man had already told her that his reason for leaving was that his feelings had not grown for her. His reason was simple, but instead of accepting it and beginning the grieving and healing process, she insisted that there must have been another reason which she must uncover. She spent a year reliving their final weekend over and over in her head, trying to pinpoint what she had done wrong or what she could have done differently. She internalized the blame, thinking "maybe it was because I was not enough of this or enough of that." But in doing so, she was only delaying her healing. She was like a detective who refused to close the case. It was like an open wound that she refused to let heal. She used all her energy looking for clues, rather than allowing for closure and acceptance.

Islamic Belief in Divine Decree

We have in our faith the conviction that some things are not meant to be and that God always knows best; to accept this Reality will accelerate healing significantly.

The Prophet said, regarding Allah's Decree (Qadr):

"The Pens have been lifted and the pages have dried." (Sahih al-Tirmidhi 2516)

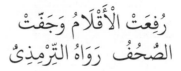

Belief in Divine destiny is essential. But it does not mean being passive. It does not mean inaction. It means we do our *absolute best*, but accept the outcome, as the Divine decree. Allah tells us in the Quran: "...perhaps you hate a thing and it is good for you, and perhaps you love a thing and it is bad for you. And Allah knows, while you do not know." (Quran 2:216)

This principle is life-changing. This understanding gives us miraculous peace, but it requires certainty in two things. It requires certainty in God's infinite knowledge/wisdom, and certainty in God's infinite mercy. God knows what we do not know. He knows the unseen, the future, and every element of the past. He knows what is best for us and what can destroy us. God is high above any analogy, but imagine a child who is desperate to play with a knife. That child may be devastated when the mother takes away the knife. But the child does not realize that the mother knows what the child does not. The mother also has immense love and mercy for the child. And the mother is acting out of that love and mercy–even when the child does not see it. Even when the child sees only deprivation because the child didn't get what they *wanted*. The mother's actions are out of mercy. And God's mercy is infinitely more than the mother's mercy for her child. Sometimes God takes things away from us, not to hurt us, but to save us. Having firm conviction of this Reality, will enable our healing.

"What ifs" Opens the Door of Shaytan

The Prophet (pbuh) said:

الْمُؤْمِنُ الْقَوِىُّ خَيْرٌ وَأَحَبُّ إِلَى اللَّهِ مِنَ الْمُؤْمِنِ الضَّعِيفِ وَفِي كُلِّ خَيْرٌ احْرِصْ عَلَى مَا يَنْفَعُكَ وَاسْتَعِنْ بِاللَّهِ وَلاَ تَعْجِزْ فَإِنْ أَصَابَكَ شَيْءٌ فَلاَ تَقُلْ لَوْ أَنِّى فَعَلْتُ كَذَا وَكَذَا وَلَكِنْ قُلْ قَدَّرَ اللَّهُ وَمَا شَاءَ فَعَلَ فَإِنَّ لَوْ تَفْتَحُ عَمَلَ الشَّيْطَانِ

*"The strong believer is better and more beloved to Allah than the weak believer, although both are good. Strive for that which will benefit you, seek the help of Allah, and do not feel helpless. **If anything befalls you, do not say, 'if only I had done such and such', rather say 'Qaddara Allahu wa ma sha'a fa'al (Allah has decreed and whatever He wills, He does).' For (saying) 'If' opens (the door) to the deeds of Satan."(Sunan Ibn Majah Vol. 1, Book 1, Hadith 79)*

This hadith contains a very powerful principle for healing and internal peace. "If" opens the door of Shaytan. This refers to the rumination on events from the past that we didn't like. This also refers to overthinking every outcome or action we have taken. We must learn from our past, but we must balance that lesson with the understanding that things happen for a reason. Even when we fail. Even when we don't live up to our own standards and the standards of others. We must take a step back and realize that even our failures have a purpose. Even our losses and our let downs. As human beings, we only see one tiny piece of the greater puzzle of life. Our vision is so limited. So we must take the lesson and move on. When we begin to overthink or hyperfocus on "if such and such", we only paralyze ourselves and open the doors of shaytan in our mind. Instead, repeat the words "*Qaddara Allahu wa ma sha'a fa'al*" on the tongue and in the heart. Tell yourself that Allah has knowingly willed this situation for your benefit, that His wisdom is Divine, and that there is certainly a reason He has only yet to reveal.

Also remember that even failure can teach us so much. First, failure teaches us humility and acceptance that we are not perfect. And that is okay. If we never failed, we would never learn the essential skill of self-compassion: being kind to ourselves and allowing ourselves the permission to be human. Failure also teaches us how to do better, and be better, next time. Research even finds that kids who don't experience failure become more reluctant to take on challenges. Failing and getting back up, builds courage and character. Failure also trains us to trust God. When a situation doesn't work out the way we want, we are forced to accept God's will, above our own.

DECISIONS BY ALLAH VS. BY THE SELF

One of the best ways to protect ourselves from these painful "if only" ruminations about the past, is by making decisions and taking actions *by Allah*, rather than *by the nafs* (self).

Taking decisions "by" Allah means that we go to God for direction and guidance in the action or decision. It means realizing that we do not know the best way, and so we ask God for guidance and help in making that decision or taking that action. This is where istikhara comes in. But it also requires a deep humility regarding our own abilities to know and act. And a deep trust in God *while* deciding and acting.

Taking actions by the nafs (self) means that we rely on ourselves to "know what's best". We rely on our own abilities and on our own knowledge when making decisions and taking action. This is extremely dangerous, as it is like driving a car while blindfolded. We will crash. But another result of making decisions and taking action by the self, is that we will always second guess that decision and will always be haunted by "what if's".

Belief and trust in Divine decree is a powerful tool of healing and a potent antidote to overthinking.

Barrier 6:
Idealizing the Object of Loss

Another factor that delays healing is idealizing the object of loss. This means forgetting anything negative about the object of loss and only remembering the positive. It is ironic and tragic that when we have something, we often focus on the negative parts of it and ignore the positive. Then when we lose something, we do the opposite: we fixate on, and exaggerate, the positive aspects. Both of these habits are unhealthy; the first habit leads to ingratitude and unhappiness when we have something. And the second habit leads to delayed healing when we lose it.

Idealizing an object of loss is a trick our mind plays on us. We may even overlook or deny abusive treatment from the past, when we fall prey to this trap. Psychologist Guy Winch often suggested that his clients keep a list of all the bad qualities of the individual who broke their heart.

He discusses a case where a woman was remarried to a good man, but continued to have feelings for her abusive ex-husband. Winch explains that one of the reasons why this happens is that the mind blurs out, or even erases, all the negative things, and then exaggerates the positive. He explains that we may even *create* good things about the object of loss. So he asked his clients to write down what that person was actually like. And every time their mind starts to play that trick, he tells them to take out the list and read it. This helps bring the person back to reality.

Barrier 7: Suppression

The next factor that delays healing is the suppression of emotion. Guy Winch explains that suppressing an emotion doesn't make it go away–it "supersizes it". In other words, when you just cover up a gunshot wound with a bandage, it doesn't make the wound go away. It only makes it worse. Suppression of emotion often turns into bitterness or toxic resentment. Like a volcano, the things we suppress don't just disappear. Eventually they explode. And if it does not eventually explode, it may slowly implode. Our suppressed emotions can slowly destroy us from the *inside*. Unprocessed negative emotion can turn into illness–both physical and psychological. Suppressed emotion or unhealed trauma can manifest as mental illness, panic attacks, chronic pain, digestive issues, migraine, ulcers, and even cancer.

Studies have found that even physical pain can be healed through compassionate awareness and acceptance. In other words, accepting the pain without judgment or resistance can actually lessen the level of physical pain we experience. One experimenter found, "Paradoxically, when we accept the pain and hold it in kind awareness, the pain often lessens, simply by changing our response to the pain." The same principle applies to emotional pain.

And yet, many of us continue to suppress our emotions for various reasons:

Culture

There are many cultures that encourage the suppression of emotion–especially negative emotion. Particularly for a woman, there is often the toxic notion that she should be able to "drink poison and keep a smile on her face". The woman is taught to be the "sacrificial lamb" of the whole family. Her aspirations, her needs, her pain, her feelings are to be put aside "for the sake of the family or kids". While noble sacrifice is praised in our religion, oppression is not. Staying quiet about abuse or injustice is not from our deen (religion). And doing it "for the sake of the kids" often backfires because children who grow up in abusive or poisonous homes suffer most. Studies show that they often suffer from mental health issues such as depression, anxiety and even suicidality. By staying in an abusive relationship, our children may also get the message that abuse is acceptable. The cycle of abuse continues long after we are gone.

Fear of Rejection

Sometimes we suppress our emotions out of fear of being rejected or misunderstood. But, by suppressing what we feel and want and need, we also suppress joy. We suppress the opportunity to experience deep connection and fulfillment. Our fear of rejection can actually end up isolating us.

Misunderstanding Forgiveness

Sometimes we suppress our emotions due to a false concept of forgiveness. First, there is the false notion that forgiveness means to "turn the other cheek". In other words, some people believe that to forgive means to allow the mistreatment to continue. Forgiveness does *not* mean being passive about ongoing injustice. Forgiveness means letting go of what has happened *in the past*, while stopping the injustice from continuing *into the future. We can let go of the past, while working to change the future.*

Another misunderstanding that exists regarding forgiveness is that you must learn to love the oppressor. This is false. It is possible that an oppressor may redeem themselves so completely that you *do* learn to love them. For example, Omar (RA) transformed from being an enemy of the Prophet (pbuh) to being one of his dearest friends. *But this is not necessarily the case.* Sometimes healing does not mean loving or even wishing well for the abuser. Sometimes the most healing thing you can do is to "let go and let God": to find peace in knowing that Allah is the *Most Just.* And, therefore, letting go of the anger or need for revenge, because you know that Allah will take care of it, *on your behalf.* That is freedom. And that is healing.

I met a woman recently after a seminar who was in extreme distress. She was literally shaking. I stepped aside to speak to her and I learned that all her rage was for one reason. She had believed that she must "forgive" her abuser by praying for him. As a result, she was actually suppressing a mountain of unprocessed pain and anger. And it was destroying her. She was trembling in her anguish.

Misunderstanding Sabr

Another reason many people suppress emotion is due to the previously mentioned misunderstanding of what sabr is. So many people have not been able to go through a healthy grieving process because of a false notion of sabr. Sabr does not mean being emotionless. Remember, Yaqoob (AS) had "sabrun jameel" (beautiful, ideal patience) and yet he also cried until he went blind after he lost Yusuf (AS). And the Prophet Muhammad (pbuh) grieved after the death of Khadijah (RA) and those closest to him.

Grief is part of being human. And the grieving process is part of healing. Often, when grief or sadness is not processed properly, it turns into toxic anger. It is like hiding food in a kitchen drawer for weeks, months, or even years. It may start off as a sandwich or a delicious cheesecake, but soon it turns poisonous. This is what can happen to us inside.

Unresolved emotion can turn toxic. The grief is not toxic; the sadness is not toxic. The *unresolved* grief and sadness are toxic. These emotions just need to be resolved. We need to feel them. We need to get through them, in order to get out, on the other side. We may need therapy to heal. But when it is suppressed, it can poison us, as it turns to rage. Or it can harden us. Or make us numb.

And this rage may not only be directed at the world–but also at *God Himself.* We need to stop having feelings about our feelings. Often, when we are sad, we don't just allow ourselves to be sad. We are *mad* that we are *sad.*

We don't just feel mad; we feel *bad* about being *mad*. We don't allow ourselves to resolve the emotion, because we layer each emotion with emotion about the emotion. We don't just let ourselves feel and work through the emotion; we judge the emotion.

In order to heal, we need to give ourselves, and others, permission to feel, without judgment or resistance. Only then, can true healing happen. There is nothing shameful about being human. Allah is the One who designed us to be human and He does not make mistakes. We must have enough compassion with ourselves to allow for the human process that Allah designed. The Prophet (pbuh) said that tears are mercy placed in the hearts of the believers. We must accept that mercy. Use it. Heal. And then rise again.

Barrier 8: Picking the Scab

Like any physical wound, our emotional wounds need to be addressed in order for them to heal. But once we have addressed the wound itself, we should not "pick the scab". In a physical wound, the scab is a protective measure that is part of the healing process. It protects the wound from bacteria and further harm or infection. When we consistently pick that scab, we delay the healing process. Similarly, certain behaviors end up "picking the scab" of our emotional wounds.

Cyberstalking

One common way that we "pick the scab" and sabotage our own healing is by cyberstalking the object of loss. It may seem harmless, but unfortunately, it is not. We end up delaying our own healing by stalking an ex-partner online. And with social media, it has become increasingly easy to monitor very personal aspects of another person's life. Today, we don't even need to hire a private investigator. We only need a device and an internet connection. And no one has to know. This is like a drug addict taking a little bit of the drug, every once in a while. Not just metaphorically–but literally. Brain scans show that when a person is "in love", the same dopamine rich areas of the brain are activated, as with cocaine. When that attachment is broken, we will literally experience withdrawal symptoms, due to the sudden drop in dopamine. Like a drug addict, we must go through a period of detoxification from the drug. When an addict is going through detox, they are blocked completely from the drug. Detox is a painful process, but it is necessary to break an addiction and heal. What would happen if an alcoholic constantly took sips of alcohol every day? Would they be able to break their addiction? The same happens when we stalk an ex-partner.

A heroin addict stays clear of heroin. An alcoholic stays clear of alcohol. And a person healing from a love addiction must also stay clear of the object of loss. Constantly "checking up" on them may give a temporary fix, but in the long run, it only feeds the addiction and prolongs the healing and detoxification process. It is self-sabotage. In this case, it would be necessary to go "cold turkey" and block, delete, unfriend. Our well-being must be more important than our curiosity. We must be very strict, as we would with a drug addiction. It is also important to recognize that when we are stalking someone online, the image we see is a photoshopped version of the person and their life.

Keeping the Pain Fresh

When a loved one passes away, a healthy grieving process is necessary for healing. But after a person has grieved properly, it is important not to keep opening the wound. This can happen through excessive reminders of the lost loved one. Moving on does not mean you have "forgotten" your loved one. The most beautiful way to honor those who have passed away is to make duaa for them. Some of these duaas may even reach them and benefit them in their grave.

Barrier 9:
Depending on Ourselves

Another mistake that delays healing while we are in pain, is depending on ourselves–rather than Allah. We may find a false sense of comfort in the illusion of control and in the self-deception of the "I got this" mentality. The truth is that none of us have "got this". We cannot get through anything on our own. In fact, one of the duaas which the Prophet (pbuh) often made was: "Do not leave me to myself for the blink of an eye." The blink of an eye is not a very long time and yet the best of creation, asked not to be left to himself–even for a moment. He understood better than any of us how desperately he needed Allah's assistance and support. *Self-reliance is a dangerous trap. Divine reliance is the path to healing.* And turning to Allah is the fastest way to heal. Tears are not weakness–they are mercy. Quran is medicine. Duaa is salvation. Prostration is recovery, and the last third of the night is our emergency room. Cry to Allah and you will heal. Break to Allah and He will mend your heart.

Some people do not turn to Allah for help because they assume that the test of God is like the test of a professor. When a professor hands you a test, you are on your own. You are not allowed to raise your hand and ask for help. That would be "cheating". Sometimes when we are being tested in life, we assume the same about Allah. We think we are "on our own" in the test. We think that being "strong" or "passing the test" means we have to harden up and rely on our own means. Allah is not like a professor. In fact, one of the reasons Allah gives us the test is *in order* for us to "raise our hand" and ask for help. The *purpose* of the test is for us to turn to Allah and ask for help. This is our elevation. By turning to Allah and depending on Him alone, we are promoted in our station with Him.

Even when our pain is self-inflicted or due to our own mistakes or sins, turning to Allah and depending on Him is still the antidote. Redemption becomes our cure and our healing.

Barrier 10: Absence of Social Support

While we know that Allah is the Ultimate Source of all healing and salvation, God assists us through tools (asbaab) in this life. Social support is one of those powerful factors that aid in healing. The support could be from a therapist, teacher, scholar, family or friend. The power of social support is also a testament to how important we can be in the healing process of another person. Our words can help heal, or they can destroy, another person. While we, ourselves, cannot be the *source* of healing or salvation for another person, we can become either a tool, or a deadly weapon, in another person's healing process.

One shocking study took 500 women with breast lumps and followed their prognosis. Those who had a stressful life event had no effect on whether the lump was malignant. Those who were emotionally isolated had no effect on whether the lump was malignant. But those who had a stressful event *and* were emotionally isolated, were ***nine times*** more likely to have their lump diagnosed as malignant.

Healthy social support is a deep blessing, but what can we do if we don't have it? First and foremost, with or without social support, we should always turn to Allah. Allah will constantly be there to support us, if we turn to Him. And we can also ask Allah to send good people who can help support us. This is not a weakness in iman (faith) or tawakkul (trust in

God). Prophet Musa (AS) asked Allah to send his brother Haroon (AS) with him as a support.

The Quran tells us Musa (AS) said: "O my Lord! Expand my chest; ease my task for me, and remove the impediment from my speech, so they may understand what I say. And give me a minister from my family, Haroon, my brother. Add to my strength through him, and make him share my task, that we may praise you much and remember You much. Indeed, You are ever-Seeing." (Quran 20: 25-35)

STEP THREE:

Treating the Wound

Emotional Power: A Psychological First Aid Kit

Most people have a strong concept of physical healing. If we break a bone or suffer from a knife wound, we have a good understanding of the process necessary for healing. We know that we need to get treatment and see a doctor. We have a first-aid kit. But when it comes to an emotional and spiritual first-aid kit, many of us fall short.

Once we diagnose the root cause of our pain, and unlearn the toxic myths and habits that block healing, we can begin to move forward towards emotional and spiritual recovery. Pain is an inevitable part of life. But Allah does not leave us alone in our tests. He gives us the tools and the help to heal and even thrive through our challenges.

The Prophet (pbuh) said,

"Every disease has a cure. If a cure is applied to the disease, it is relieved by the permission of Allah Almighty." (Sahīh Muslim 2204)

عَنْ جَابِرٍ عَنْ رَسُولِ اللَّهِ صَلَّى اللَّهُ عَلَيْهِ وَسَلَّمَ أَنَّهُ قَالَ لِكُلِّ دَاءٍ دَوَاءٌ فَإِذَا أُصِيبَ دَوَاءُ الدَّاءِ بَرَأَ بِإِذْنِ اللَّهِ عَزَّ وَجَلَّ

Pain is real. But so are the tools to heal it. We are told to take action to improve our own situation and prevent pain from turning into prolonged *suffering*. We were meant to be *tested* in this life. But we are not meant to sit passively and *suffer*. And just like there are factors which hinder healing, there are also psychological and spiritual tools that support and even expedite the healing process.

Tool 1: Advice of a Resilience Expert

A significant amount of research has been done on the psychological factors that build emotional and mental strength. One wellbeing and resilience expert, Lucy Hone, had her work hit very close to home. After spending years training others on resilience, Lucy Hone was tested. When her daughter was only 12 years old, she died suddenly in a car accident while the family was on vacation. Hone, who is also the author of *Resilient Grieving*, describes three things that got her through the tragedy.

1. CHANGE YOUR EXPECTATIONS

Lucy explains how she never asked, "why me?" about her tragedy. She understood that terrible things happen to everyone, so her thinking was more "why not me?". She describes how we live in a world where people have forgotten this reality and instead live feeling *entitled* to a perfect life. We spend hours every day watching people's "perfect lives" displayed online, and many of us fall for the delusion. And so when difficult things do happen, many people end up feeling "discriminated against". If you believe that others have a perfect life and that you are also entitled to a perfect life, when challenges occur, you will feel like "it's not fair". By maintaining a realistic understanding and expectation of life, Lucy was better able to cope with the tragedy of losing her daughter.

Ironically, one of the deepest mistakes we make is that we hold *high expectations from dunya and low expectations from Allah*. We expect this life to be perfect–a worldly paradise. We expect it to last and to give us everything we desire.

And when it comes to Allah, we often think negatively. When we are tested, we assume He is punishing us. When we don't get what we want, we assume Allah is withholding gifts from us. With Dunya, we expect love and generosity, and to never be let down.

With Allah, we see only His wrath, but not His loving mercy. We see that He is "withholding" from us, rather than trusting His wisdom and love.

Expectations of Dunya:

The literal meaning of the phrase "hayat ul Dunya" is "the lower life". Absorbing that Reality will be the first step in building mental strength. There are certain truths that we understand about this world. For example, we know that we cannot control the weather. We also know that the weather will never stay perfect. There will inevitably be times of bad weather that last days, weeks, months or even years. The weather of our lives may be the same.

Expectations of Allah:

"Allah the Most High said, 'I am as My servant thinks (expects) I am. I am with him when he mentions Me. If he mentions Me to himself, I mention him to Myself; and if he mentions Me in an assembly, I mention him in an assembly greater than it. If he draws near to Me a hand's length, I draw near to him an arm's length. And if he comes to Me walking, I go to him at speed.'" (Hadith Qudsi).

The first step to emotional strength is having a realistic expectation of Dunya and a positive expectation of Allah.

2. CHANGE YOUR FOCUS

As humans, we are hardwired to tune into any possible threat as a protective measure. If a tiger is charging at us, it would not be adaptive to focus on a beautiful tree. But the problem is that many of us still live in this part of the brain where everything is coded as a "tiger". So there is a constant high alert and chronic stress (fight-or-flight) response. During the stress response, high levels of cortisol are released. In order to help us confront a temporary threat, cortisol works to raise blood pressure, increase blood sugar, suppress immunity and slow digestion. But when our body interprets most of our life as a threat, the stress response can become chronic and cause many health issues including anxiety, depression, heart disease, diabetes, and even cancer.

Lucy describes how she survived by shifting her focus. Instead of focusing on what she could not change or what was negative, she consciously chose to tune into the good. She said to herself: "You cannot get swallowed up by this—you've got so much to live for. Don't lose what you have to what you have lost."

In psychology, it's called "benefit-finding".

She writes:

"In my new world, it involved trying to find things to be grateful for. At least, our dear girl hadn't died from a terrible, long, drawn-out illness. She died suddenly, instantly, sparing us and her that pain. We also had a huge amount of social support from our family and friends to help us through. Most of all, we still had two beautiful boys who needed us and deserved to have as normal a life as we could possibly give them. When you're going through a difficult time, you might need a reminder or permission to feel grateful. In our kitchen, we've got a neon-pink poster that says, 'Accept the good'."

She advises: "Whatever you do, make an intentional, deliberate, ongoing effort to tune in to what's good in your world."

There is a concept called "collateral beauty". "Collateral damage" refers to the injury inflicted on something other than an intended target. "Collateral beauty" is the opposite. It is the beauty that surrounds the pain. Lucy explains that she survived her loss by actively *looking* for it every day. And what you focus on, grows. When you live your life looking for the good and focusing on it, it increases. You *feel* rich. You *feel* thankful. When you actively and consciously practice gratitude, you become grateful. This means seeking out things to be grateful for. Psychological studies found that writing down just three things you are grateful for every day, significantly reduces depression.

Albert Einstein once said, "There are two ways to live your life. One is as though nothing is a miracle. The other is as though *everything* is a miracle." We choose which way we will see our world. We choose which lens we will wear. The dark or the light.

Allah says,

"Indeed with hardship is ease."
(Quran 94:6)

إِنَّ مَعَ الْعُسْرِ يُسْرًا ۝

So at any given moment, we all have both difficulties *and* blessings. They come *together*. We choose which to focus on. And *that* choice makes all the difference.

3. ASK YOURSELF "IS THIS HELPFUL OR HURTFUL?"

After the death of her daughter, Lucy Hone describes how she would often find herself "poring over old photos" that were making her more and more upset. At some point she began to ask herself this crucial question for healing and resilience: "Is this helping me or hurting me"? We often have patterns of thinking and behavior that are in fact sabotaging our own healing. For example, when Lucy was deciding whether to attend the trial and see the driver who killed her daughter, Lucy asked herself this question. She decided to stay away because she knew it would only hurt her. This question is essential in everything we do. We must ask ourselves if a particular way of thinking, habit, or action will help or hurt. We must be conscious and take an *active* role in our own healing. This is part of self-compassion.

Tool 2: Every Moment Make Three Decisions

Life coach, Tony Robbins explains that in every moment we must make three decisions to improve the quality of our lives. We must choose what we will focus on, we must decide what meaning we attach to it, and then we must decide which action to take.

1. WHAT YOU WILL FOCUS ON

Every discussion about well-being and emotional health will always emphasize focus. Focus is everything. It is the direction we fixate and the direction we move. Focus determines what is most prominent in our lives. Focus colors our whole life. We choose whether that color is dark or light.

2. WHAT IT MEANS

The second crucial decision we must make is what meaning we will assign to what is happening in our lives. Do we believe what Allah does is good for us? Do you see goodness in what Allah chooses? Even if it isn't what you want. Do you believe that your life is happening *to* you or *for* you?

The Prophet (pbuh) said:

عَجَبًا لِأَمْرِ الْمُؤْمِنِ إِنَّ أَمْرَهُ كُلَّهُ خَيْرٌ وَلَيْسَ ذَاكَ لِأَحَدٍ إِلَّا لِلْمُؤْمِنِ إِنْ أَصَابَتْهُ سَرَّاءُ شَكَرَ فَكَانَ خَيْرًا لَهُ وَإِنْ أَصَابَتْهُ ضَرَّاءُ صَبَرَ فَكَانَ خَيْرًا لَهُ

"The matters of a believer are amazing, for there is good for them in every matter; and this is not the case with anyone except the believer. If something of good/happiness befalls them, they are thankful, so it is good for them. And if something of (perceived) harm befalls them, they show patience, so it is good for them." (Sahih Muslim 2999)

The Prophet (pbuh) also said:

"I am amazed by the believer. Verily, Allah does not decree anything for the believer except what is good for him." (Musnad Ahmad 12495)

عَجِبْتُ لِلْمُؤْمِنِ إِنَّ اللَّهَ لَا يَقْضِي لِلْمُؤْمِنِ قَضَاءً إِلَّا كَانَ خَيْرًا لَهُ

We learn from the words of the Prophet (pbuh) that, if we are believers, every matter which comes our way is actually good for us. So the believer should have hope and assign a positive meaning to all they encounter in life. And this makes all the difference.

3. WHICH ACTION YOU WILL TAKE

Many people believe that "knowledge is power". But Tony Robbins explains that "knowledge is not power, it's potential power." He emphasizes that "execution trumps knowledge every day of the week."

In other words, it's good to learn something new or feel inspired. But unless we put that knowledge into *action*, it won't help us. Allah tells us again and again in the Quran "those who believe *and* do righteous deeds." It is not enough to just believe. We must put that belief into action. Whether it is in the realm of dunya or deen, many people know what needs to be done, but still do nothing about it.

Robbins says he refuses to "learn something or make a decision about something valuable without making [him]self do something in the moment that commits [him] to follow through." Robbins explains that "everyone who wants change should do the same...Because if you hesitate, a million distractions will come up and you'll lose your momentum."

Tool 3: Invest in Relationships

Harvard University conducted the longest longitudinal study on happiness. In this study, researchers followed participants over a span of almost 80 years, measuring their level of happiness, along with various other factors, such as wealth, career, health, and relationships. After almost 80 years of studying the lives and happiness of participants, the results were fascinating.

The study found that close relationships, more than money or fame, are what keep people happy throughout their lives. The study further found that it is our relationships that help protect us from life's discontents, help to delay mental and physical decline, and are better predictors of long and happy lives than social class, IQ, or even genes.

Despite this reality, we live in a culture that pushes the very opposite. Sacrificing family and other close relationships is often seen as necessary to get ahead in a career or to be "successful". There is the notion that getting ahead in the realm of money or fame will make us happy. Our society pushes this material definition of success. You are told that if you can be rich and famous, you'll be happy. If you can excel in your career, you'll be happy. This is how we're sold happiness. But this study found that the quality of happiness was actually related to the quality of relationships. But what's even more fascinating is that they also found that the strength of their relationships was also directly related to physical health as well. Robert Waldinger, director of the study and professor of Psychiatry at Harvard Medical School explains: "The people who were the most satisfied in their relationships at age 50 were the healthiest at age 80."

Tool 4: Self-Compassion

Studies have found that even physical pain can be lessened through compassionate awareness and acceptance. By accepting our physical and emotional pain without judgment or resistance, the pain itself is reduced. "Paradoxically, when we accept the pain and hold it in kind awareness, the pain often lessens, simply by changing our response to the pain," explains Glenn R. Schiraldi, author of *The Adverse Childhood Experiences Recovery Workbook*, *The Resilience Workbook*, *The Post-Traumatic Stress Disorder Sourcebook*, and *the* founder of Resilience Training International.

Tool 5: Service

Service to others (prosocial behavior) has been found to be among the most effective ways to increase happiness and well-being. The American Journal of Preventive Medicine released research that finds volunteering regularly protects against depression and promotes happiness and longevity. "Our results show that volunteerism among older adults doesn't just strengthen communities, but enriches our own lives by strengthening our bonds to others, helping us feel a sense of purpose and well-being, and protecting us from feelings of loneliness, depression, and hopelessness," explains lead study author Dr. Eric Kim, of the Chan School of Public Health at Harvard University.

The tradition of service is deeply rooted in Islam. The Prophet (pbuh) said:

عَنِ ابْنِ عُمَرَ أَنَّ النَّبِيَّ صَلَّى اللَّهُ عَلَيْهِ وَسَلَّمَ قَالَ أَحَبُّ
النَّاسِ إِلَى اللَّهِ أَنْفَعُهُمْ لِلنَّاسِ وَأَحَبُّ الْأَعْمَالِ إِلَى اللَّهِ سُرُورٌ
تُدْخِلُهُ عَلَى مُسْلِمٍ أَوْ تَكْشِفُ عَنْهُ كُرْبَةً أَوْ تَقْضِى عَنْهُ
دِينًا أَوْ تَطْرُدُ عَنْهُ جُوعًا وَلَأَنْ أَمْشِيَ مع أَخٍ فِى حَاجَةٍ أَحَبُّ
إِلَىَّ مِنْ أَنْ أَعْتَكِفَ فِى هَذَا الْمَسْجِدِ يَعْنِى مَسْجِدَ الْمَدِينَةِ
شَهْرًا وَمَنْ كَفَّ غَضَبَهُ سَتَرَ اللهُ عَوْرَتَهُ وَمَنْ كَظَمَ غَيْظَهُ
وَلَوْ شَاءَ أَنْ يُمْضِيَهُ أَمْضَاهُ مَلَأَ اللهُ عَزَّ وَجَلَّ قَلْبَهُ أَمْنًا يَوْمَ
الْقِيَامَةِ وَمَنْ مَشَى مع أخيه فِى حَاجَةٍ حَتَّى أَثْبَتَهَا لَهُ أَثْبَتَ
اللهُ عَزَّ وَجَلَّ قَدَمَهُ عَلَى الصِّرَاطِ يَوْمَ تَزِلُّ فِيهِ الْأَقْدَامُ

"The most beloved people to Allah are those who are most beneficial to people. The most beloved deed to Allah is to make a Muslim happy, or to remove one of his troubles, or to forgive his debt, or to feed his hunger. That I walk with a brother regarding a need is more beloved to me than that I seclude myself in this mosque in Medina for a month. Whoever swallows his anger, then Allah will conceal his faults. Whoever suppresses his rage, even though he could fulfill his anger if he wished, then Allah will secure his heart on the Day of Resurrection. Whoever walks with his brother regarding a need until he secures it for him, then Allah Almighty will make his footing firm across the bridge on the Day when the footings are shaken." (Sahih, al-Mu'jam al-Awsat 6026)

These words of the Prophet (pbuh) are so powerful because he explains that he prefers to help someone in need than even to do itikaf (seclusion in the masjid) in Masjid Al-Nabawi of Madina.

Tool 6: Platinum Rule

As we review the Quran and sunnah, we learn a powerful principle: Allah will treat us like we treat others. So this leads us to an important principle. The "Golden Rule" says: "Treat others as you would like to be treated." In Islam, we have another rule; let's call it the "Platinum Rule": "Treat others as you would like *God* to treat you."

The Prophet (pbuh) said: "Whoever is not merciful to people will not be shown mercy from Allah." (al-Mu'jam al-Kabīr 3847)

When Allah sent verses instructing Abu Bakr (RA) to pardon his relative who had spread the slander about his daughter Ayesha (RA), Allah said: "Those who have been graced with bounty and plenty should not swear that they will [no longer] give to kinsmen, the poor, those who emigrated in God's way: *let them pardon and forgive. Do you not wish that God should forgive you? God is most forgiving and merciful."* (Quran 24:22)

Abu Bakr (RA) had been financially supporting the relative that was spreading the slander about his daughter. Yet, after hearing this verse, Abu Bakr (RA) not only continued the financial support he was giving, he increased it.

It is also interesting to note that when Musa (AS) was at his lowest point (after accidentally killing a man and fleeing Pharoah), he came to the aid of two women with their animal. It is by Divine design that so often the fastest way to pull ourselves up when we are down, is to help pull up another person.

Tool 7: Living with Purpose

We spend our lives chasing happiness. We live in a world that teaches us to put ourselves at the center. And to make our own pleasure the ultimate goal. We are told that if we do this, if we make our own personal happiness the goal, we will finally reach it. But happiness is not a destination. It comes along the way. If we make our own personal pleasure the ultimate goal of our lives, we will never be pleased. But if we make *being pleasing to God* the ultimate goal, God will make us pleased. Our life on this earth is not about the pursuit of happiness. It is about the pursuit of meaning and purpose. And this is the true essence of a good life.

Allah tells us:

"Whoever does good, whether male or female, and is a believer, We will surely bless them with a good life, and We will certainly reward them according to the best of their deeds." (Quran 16:97)

مَنْ عَمِلَ صَالِحًا مِنْ ذَكَرٍ أَوْ
أُنْثَى وَهُوَ مُؤْمِنٌ فَلَنُحْيِيَنَّهُ
حَيَاةً طَيِّبَةً وَلَنَجْزِيَنَّهُمْ
أَجْرَهُمْ بِأَحْسَنِ مَا كَانُوا
يَعْمَلُونَ ﴿٩٧﴾

This ayah describes how to achieve the true meaning of a "good life". It is a contented life, and it is achieved when we live for a higher purpose, according to our morals and principles.

Even in psychological studies, it has been demonstrated, for example, that having children does *not* increase happiness; in fact, it actually *decreases* happiness. But having children increases *meaning*. And increasing meaning gives us true contentment and increases overall well-being. Several studies across cultures early in the Covid-19 pandemic found that increasing meaning had a profound effect on mental health. These studies found that increased meaning is associated with greater resilience, reduced anxiety and distress, and better functioning. Furthermore, purposely increasing meaning may bolster resilience. Researchers discovered that texting the following reflective prompt every day for one week increased "meaning salience". And participants who received this prompt showed reduced anxiety, depression, and stress compared with those receiving a neutral prompt. Those who received the prompt also coped better with social isolation:

Prompt:

"As you go through the next few hours of your day, please remember to attend to the activities that you are engaging in. In addition, make sure to think about how meaningful each of these moments are. We will ask about each of these daily moments when you reflect on your day later tonight."

The Heart's Medicine: A Spiritual First Aid Kit

There are many psychological resources that help us heal, but even more powerful than all of these are the spiritual resources given to us by God and His Messenger (pbuh). These potent tools can transform our lives and the way we respond to pain, but only when applied consistently. Knowledge is power—but only when lived. Only when that knowledge is integrated internally and externally. One of my teachers used to say, "Knowledge is not *informational*. It is *transformational*." Some people can memorize the entire Quran, but it has no effect on their heart or their life. Some people even end up using religious knowledge to control others. For these people, worship is only ritual, and knowledge is just a weapon to dominate. For them, learning only makes them more harsh. But if spiritual knowledge has made us harder inside, it means that knowledge has not penetrated the heart. When the light of God truly enters our hearts, it changes us. It softens us and transforms our actions and our lives.

Tool 1: Divine Prescription for a Heavy Heart

Allah has said:

> *"And indeed We know that your chest is constrained by what they say. So exalt [God] with praise of your Lord and be of those who prostrate [to Him]." (Quran 15:97-98)*

وَلَقَدْ نَعْلَمُ أَنَّكَ يَضِيقُ صَدْرُكَ بِمَا يَقُولُونَ ۝ فَسَبِّحْ بِحَمْدِ رَبِّكَ وَكُنْ مِنَ السَّاجِدِينَ ۝

After acknowledging the pain caused specifically by the words of others, Allah gives the antidote. "So glorify the praises of your Lord and be one of those who prostrate."

There are two fundamental parts to this Divine prescription for a broken heart. The heavy heart is caused by the creation, and so the antidote is to rise above the creation and exalt the Creator: "Glorify the praises of your Lord." And then the second part of this prescription is to prostrate—to humble ourselves and *submit* to God. This is the heart's greatest healing.

Tool 2: Gratitude

In the Quran, Allah teaches us a secret for healing and strengthening the heart during our times of grief or distress. He teaches us to reflect on all the times God has saved us in the past.

Take the example of Musa (AS). When Allah reassures Musa (AS), He reminds Musa (AS) of all the times He took care of Musa (AS) in the past. Allah says:

"And surely We had shown You favor before, when We inspired your mother with this: 'Put him into a chest, then put it into the river. The river will wash it ashore, and he will be taken by "Pharaoh", an enemy of Mine and his.' And I blessed you with lovability from Me, Oh Moses so that you would be brought up under My watchful Eye." (Quran 20:37-39)

When Allah reassures Prophet Muhammad (pbuh), He does the same. Allah says:

"Did He not find you as an orphan then sheltered you? Did He not find you unguided then guided you? And did He not find you needy then satisfy your needs?" (93:6-8)

And just before these verses, the early revelations given to the Prophet (pbuh) were "qumm": "stand" (Surat Al Muzzamil and Mudathir). So when you find yourself in distress or even falling into despair, remember the favors of Allah upon you and all the times He has saved you in the past. This will heal you. It will strengthen you. And it will allow you to "stand" again.

Gratitude is an antidote to depression and envy, and it is the cultivator of blessings. Studies have found that people with higher levels of gratitude report more optimism, positive affect, and satisfaction with life. In positive psychology research, gratitude is strongly and consistently associated with greater happiness. Gratitude helps people feel more positive emotions, relish good experiences, improve their health, deal with adversity, and build strong relationships.

Two psychologists, Dr. Robert A. Emmons of the University of California, Davis, and Dr. Michael E. McCullough of the University of Miami have done a great deal of the research on gratitude. In one study, they asked all participants to write a few sentences each week, focusing on particular topics.

One group wrote about things they were grateful for that had occurred during the week. A second group wrote about daily irritations or things that had displeased them, and the third group wrote about events that had affected them (with no emphasis on them being positive or negative). After 10 weeks, those who wrote about gratitude were more optimistic and felt better about their lives. Surprisingly, they also exercised more and had fewer visits to physicians than those who focused on sources of aggravation.

Another leading researcher in this field, Dr. Martin E. P. Seligman, tested the impact of various positive psychology interventions on 411 people, each compared with a control assignment of writing about early memories. When their week's assignment was to write and personally deliver a letter of gratitude to someone who had never been properly thanked for his or her kindness, participants immediately exhibited a huge increase in happiness scores. This impact was greater than that from any other intervention, with benefits lasting for a month.

What we focus on, grows. Practicing gratitude shifts our focus from what we don't like in our lives, to what we *do* like. And so it grows. As a result, our psychological state changes and the lens with which we process the world changes. The cliche "seeing the world through rose colored glasses" refers to this phenomenon; when a person puts on glasses that are rose-colored, the whole world looks rose colored. It looks bright and positive. But imagine a person who is always wearing dark lenses. The world will always look dark—even if it's bright. Even if the world is actually very, very beautiful, such a person will see everything as dark, because their lens is dark. Psychologically, it is a matter of changing the lens to a brighter one. And spiritually, it is a matter of *cleaning* the lens. This is part of the practice of purification of the heart. When you do this, it changes the way you see the world.

The practice of gratitude allows us to put on grateful lenses. It changes the way we view the world, and allows our radar and focus to calibrate differently. We become *calibrated* to *look* for positive things. To *look for* blessings—instead of problems and deficiencies.

And Allah gives you more. Allah says:

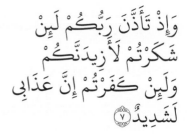

"And [remember] when your Lord proclaimed, 'If you are grateful, I will surely increase you [in favor]; but if you deny, indeed, My punishment is severe.'" (Quran 14:7)

Here, God teaches us that there is a link between gratitude and abundance. You find that this is the case even with human beings. If you want a behavior in another person to continue or to increase, should you show gratitude or ingratitude for what you've seen so far? The more you show gratitude towards that individual and what they have already done, the more that behavior will increase. This applies with our spouses. This also applies with our children, and with our colleagues and friends. When you are grateful for what the individual is already doing, it motivates them to do even more. For example, our children are not motivated by criticism. They are motivated by appreciation.

With regards to gratitude and spirituality, I learned something life changing. Many of us often feel we are not doing enough. We may feel inadequate and frustrated when we don't live up to our own expectations. Or when others (our family, friends, loved ones) do not live up to our expectations of them.

When this happens, our response is typically to focus on what's "missing" in our efforts, or in the efforts of others we care about. We focus on what's missing in hopes of increasing it. This often happens spiritually, especially when we feel disappointed in our worship during Ramadan. But what if we used a completely different approach? What if we used this Quranic approach: "If you are thankful, I will increase you." (Quran 14:7)?

Instead of focusing on what's missing in our deeds, what if we showed gratitude to Allah for the spiritual gifts He has *already* given us? Maybe we weren't able to stay up all night, but Allah allowed us to make heartfelt duaa or pray some portion of the night. Or maybe He allowed us to help another person in need or to be at the service of our family. When we show gratitude for the gifts He has given us, He gives us more. And all good comes from Allah, so we must be careful not to take credit for our own worship or good deeds. Our prayer is not a gift from us to God. It is a gift from God to us.

Gratitude is also an antidote for envy. Often what keeps us unhappy is that when we look at our own lives, we focus on our hardships, rather than our blessings. And then what makes us envious of others is that we flip the equation. With others, we focus on their blessings, but not their hardships. And social media is a dangerous platform for this skewed focus. It's a place to see the blessings of others, while hiding their hardships. When we focus on our own blessings, we no longer "feel poor" compared to others.

Tool 3: Positive Opinion of Allah and Tawakkul

Among the most important and transformative actions of the heart is *husnul than billah*: to always have a positive opinion or expectation from Allah. This manifests when we always assume the best from what God is doing. It means to always look with a positive lens at the work of God—at the actions of God in our lives and in the world. This spiritual practice completely transforms the way we respond to our lives.

Take the following example: Imagine that your mother comes to pick you up. As she starts to drive, you ask her where you're going. Imagine that your mother replies, "Don't worry, you'll see." At that point, do you panic and call the police? Of course you will not, but the question is *why not?* Why don't you panic and call for help when you don't know the route? And would it be any different if you were in a taxi and didn't know the driver? The answer is simple. The only reason you would not panic with your mother is because you *trust the driver.* Even though you *don't know the route,* and are *not in control,* you trust that your mother has your best interests in mind and you have a positive opinion of her and her actions. This is called "husnul than". You don't think that she's trying to hurt you. You don't think she's going to take you to a ditch and leave you. You know that she's doing what's best for you–even when you don't know how. You don't panic because you *trust the driver.* When we think about God in this way, we don't panic when we don't know the route He's taking with our lives. Husul than billah totally transforms the way we respond. Even when we don't understand, we won't react negatively because we are certain that God's actions are not meant to hurt us and that what He chooses is in our best interest. It means that even when I don't know the route, even when I don't see a way out, even when it looks like everything is closing in, I hold onto a very, very deeply rooted positive opinion of Allah.

It means knowing with certainty that whatever Allah is doing in my life is for my own good. This is essential and transformative. Another example of this concept is the example of a doctor. If a doctor tells you that you require surgery to save your life. You will need certainty in two things before you submit to going under the knife. You will need certainty in the doctor's *knowledge,* and certainty in the doctor's *good intentions.* If you find out that the doctor never graduated from medical school, or that the doctor is corrupt and just wants money, you will never submit to the surgery. But, if the doctor is your mother and she is the best surgeon in the country, you will submit with full confidence. Realize that God's knowledge and mercy is infinitely more than any doctor or mother.

But do we trust Him? Do we believe that He knows? And do we believe that He wants what's best for us? The answer to these questions will transform our lives and the way we respond to our trials. When we submit to the will and Divine wisdom of God, we find internal peace, even in the face of difficulty. Even in the face of disappointment. With the doctor, we submit to the reality that we are limited in our own medical knowledge and in our ability to do surgery ourselves. And yet, ironically, with the Lord of the worlds, we act as though we can know what He knows. Ironically, we are more humble with a doctor, than we are with God.

Allah is high above any analogy. His knowledge is high above any doctor and His love and mercy are infinitely greater than any mother.

Tool 4: Taqwa and Trust

When we put our trust in Allah and have consciousness of Him (taqwa), we are promised God's protection. Allah says: "Whoever has taqwa of Allah, We will make a way out for them and provide for them from places they never imagined. And whoever places their trust in Allah, Allah will be enough for them (will suffice them)." (Quran 65:2-3)

What is taqwa and how can we develop it?

Taqwa is the process of shielding oneself from displeasing Allah. It is to be cautious in all of one's affairs, out of consciousness that Allah is All-Knowing (Aleem) and All-Seeing (Baseer). Allah describes the people of Taqwa:

لَيْسَ الْبِرَّ أَنْ تُوَلُّوا وُجُوهَكُمْ قِبَلَ الْمَشْرِقِ وَالْمَغْرِبِ وَلَٰكِنَّ الْبِرَّ مَنْ آمَنَ بِاللَّهِ وَالْيَوْمِ الْآخِرِ وَالْمَلَائِكَةِ وَالْكِتَابِ وَالنَّبِيِّينَ وَآتَى الْمَالَ عَلَىٰ حُبِّهِ ذَوِي الْقُرْبَىٰ وَالْيَتَامَىٰ وَالْمَسَاكِينَ وَابْنَ السَّبِيلِ وَالسَّائِلِينَ وَفِي الرِّقَابِ وَأَقَامَ الصَّلَاةَ وَآتَى الزَّكَاةَ وَالْمُوفُونَ بِعَهْدِهِمْ إِذَا عَاهَدُوا وَالصَّابِرِينَ فِي الْبَأْسَاءِ وَالضَّرَّاءِ وَحِينَ الْبَأْسِ أُولَٰئِكَ الَّذِينَ صَدَقُوا وَأُولَٰئِكَ هُمُ الْمُتَّقُونَ ﴿١٧٧﴾

"Righteousness is not that you turn your faces toward the east or the west, but [true] righteousness is [in] one who believes in Allah, the Last Day, the angels, the Book, and the prophets and gives wealth, in spite of love for it, to relatives, orphans, the needy, the traveler, those who ask [for help], and for freeing slaves; [and who] establishes prayer and gives zakah; [those who] fulfill their promise when they promise; and [those who] are patient in poverty and hardship and during battle. Those are the ones who have been true, and it is those who are the righteous." (Quran 2:177)

In the beginning of Surat Al Baqarah, Allah gives another description of the people of Taqwa:

"This is the Book! There is no doubt about it—a guide for those mindful of Allah, who believe in the unseen, establish prayer, and donate from what We have provided for them, and who believe in what has been revealed to you O Prophet and what was revealed before you, and have sure faith in the Hereafter. It is they who are truly guided by their Lord, and it is they who will be successful." (Quran 2:2-5)

One of the descriptions of the people of taqwa are those who believe in the unseen. This is the foundation of taqwa and trust (tawakkul). We must have the ability to see through the fog, beyond the illusions. We must have the ability to see the dawn, while standing in the midst of the night. We must have the inner sight to see the calm, while standing in the middle of the storm. To see the victory, while standing in defeat.

Not after it has passed. In the *midst* of it.

Because it is *then* that the dawn, the calm, and the victory is unseen.

This ability to trust what is unseen becomes the foundation of a believer's success in this life. And thus, Allah says: "...and it is they who will be successful." (Quran 2:5)

Tawakkul, putting your full trust and reliance on Allah will save you. Allah tells us a powerful story in the Quran about a man who was threatened by Pharoah, the greatest tyrant to walk the earth. In the midst of this man's hardship, he puts his full trust in Allah, and then is saved.

Allah tells us that the man said:

"And you will remember what I [now] say to you, and I entrust my affair to Allah. Indeed, Allah is Seeing of [His] servants. So Allah protected him from the evils they plotted, and the people of Pharaoh were enveloped by the worst of punishment." (Quran 40:44-45)

فَسَتَذْكُرُونَ مَا أَقُولُ لَكُمْ وَأُفَوِّضُ أَمْرِى إِلَى اللَّهِ إِنَّ اللَّهَ بَصِيرٌ بِالْعِبَادِ ۝ فَوَقَاهُ اللَّهُ سَيِّئَاتِ مَا مَكَرُوا وَحَاقَ بِآلِ فِرْعَوْنَ سُوءُ الْعَذَابِ ۝

This man was saved by putting his affairs completely in the hands of God. And, yet, when we are put in difficult situations, many of us are desperate to take control. But, I honestly can't imagine anything more frightening. To be the one in charge of what happens to ourselves or to others. To be the one actually steering the ship of this life. What a paralyzing responsibility. What a terrifying proposition. With all our weaknesses and limitations. Our flaws and our biases. Our total blindness to what is to come in the future or what is beyond our sight or understanding.

There are people who find it frightening when Allah says,

"Allah has full power to implement His design, although most people do not know." (Quran 12:21)

وَاللَّهُ غَالِبٌ عَلَى أَمْرِهِ وَلَكِنَّ أَكْثَرَ النَّاسِ لَا يَعْلَمُونَ ۝

To me, those are some of the most comforting words. It means it's not "all on me". It means I'm *not* in charge. I'm not responsible for making things happen a certain way. It means I can lay down the weight of the world. I can lay down the weight of my fears about the future. My fears that things won't work out a particular way. It means I am not my own master. I don't decide the outcomes. And so I must submit.

And only in that submission, do I find peace. And salvation.

Tool 5: Softening in Hardship

We often believe that to be strong, we must be hard. We may even advise others going through hardship and heartbreak, to "harden up" to "be strong". But the Prophet (pbuh) defined strength very differently. He (pbuh) said,

مَثَلُ الْمُؤْمِنِ كَمَثَلِ الْخَامَةِ مِنَ الزَّرْعِ مِنْ حَيْثُ أَتَتْهَا
الرِّيحُ كَفَأَتْهَا فَإِذَا اعْتَدَلَتْ تَكَفَّأُ بِالْبَلَاءِ وَالْفَاجِرُ
كَالْأَرْزَةِ صَمَّاءَ مُعْتَدِلَةً حَتَّى يَقْصِمَهَا اللَّهُ إِذَا شَاءَ

"The example of a believer is that of a fresh tender plant; from whatever direction the wind comes, it bends it, but when the wind becomes quiet, it becomes straight again. Similarly, a believer is afflicted with calamities (but he remains patient till Allah removes his difficulties). And an impious wicked person is like a pine tree which keeps hard and straight till Allah cuts (breaks) it down when He wishes." (Sahih al-Bukhari 5644)

When you reflect carefully on this hadith, you realize a fascinating truth: *strength comes from internal softness–not hardness.* Notice what happens to the "tender plant": it bends with the wind, but does not break. The rigid pine is the one that breaks. When we are rigid in the face of hardships, we actually make ourselves *more* vulnerable and breakable. Like a volcano that suppresses pressure for years, but then it explodes.

Allah says in the Quran:

"Do not weaken and do not grieve, for you will have the upper hand, if you are [true] believers." (Quran 3:139)

وَلَا تَهِنُوا وَلَا تَحْزَنُوا
وَأَنْتُمُ الْأَعْلَوْنَ إِنْ كُنْتُمْ
مُؤْمِنِينَ ۞

This ayah in surah Al-Imran was revealed during one of the hardest times for the Prophet (pbuh) and his companions. It was revealed during the Battle of Uhud, where many believers lost their lives and the Prophet (pbuh) himself was injured.

It is fascinating to note that the word used in this ayah is "huzn". This term is often translated as "sadness". But Allah is not just saying "do not be sad". The ayah says, "do not have huzn".

The word "huzn" comes from the 3 letter root "ن ز ح". This root contains an element of hardness and harshness.

When we are faced with a hardship or challenge, our reflex may be to harden up. We may feel lost and not understand what the "right way" is. Our hardships often feel like tests that we can't find the right answers to. We may try to weather the storm by hardening inside, and relying on ourselves. But the "correct answer" is the opposite. Allah wants us to soften up. Turn to Him. Rely on Him. And ask of Him.

That is the "right answer".

See, there are two ways to face a storm. You can fight it, "curse the fates". Or you can surrender and turn to shelter. F. Scott Fitzgerald wrote: "You can be as mad as a mad dog at the way things went. You could swear, curse the fates, but when it comes to the end, you have to let go."

We often forget that Allah is Al-Rahman, the Most Merciful. But, He is also Al-Qahar (the Overpowering and Irresistible). Too often, we only hurt ourselves more by resisting the decrees of Allah. When Allah shows us His power (His 'Qahr'), our response should be to submit and accept. Not to fight. Of course, there is a time and place to take action, to do our part in bad situations. But sometimes, when there is nothing we can do to change it, our worship in that moment is to accept. This is sabr. Even when it hurts, we do not complain *against* Allah's decree. But, remember, those who were nearest to Allah, complained *to* Allah of their grief. They turned to Allah for help and healing. This is fundamentally different from complaining *about* Allah, which is to complain against the decision of Allah: To say, "why me?" "It's not fair!" "How could you do this to me, God?!"

When we complain against Allah, we are screaming into the storm, cursing the wind and rain. Doing this does not change the weather or lessen the storm. It does not destroy the storm, but only allows the storm to destroy us. Denying that the storm is there will also not make it go away. The only way to survive a storm is to accept that the storm is there and to find shelter.

Tool 6: Duaa

The only true shelter in the storm is God. Breaking to Allah is the only way to heal. Do not make duaa as if you've only just met Allah. When you call out to Him, broken, begging, and on your knees, remember He is the same One who saved you before. He is the same One who found you desperate and saved you. The One who found you broken and healed you. The One who found you needy and gave you. The One who found you terrified and protected you. The One who found you empty and filled you. The One who found you lost and guided you. And the one who found you weak and strengthened you.

Many people do not turn to Allah when they are tested because they believe that they must handle their tests all on their own. So when Allah tests them, they end up suffering alone. They carry the burden on their own. They may ask Allah for "strength" or "sabr"; but they don't ask for help or relief. They rely on themselves—their own "strength" and "abilities". They think: "I got this." "I'm strong." "I can do this."

But that's the wrong answer.

When we turn to Allah and ask for help, we fulfill the very purpose of the storm. Sometimes the very purpose of the test is to push us to ask God for help. The very purpose of the storm is to push us to shelter. The shelter of Allah. To turn to Him in total need and humility. That's tadaru' (humility).

"Whenever We sent a prophet to a town, We took up its people in suffering and adversity, in order that they might learn humility." (Quran 7:94)	وَمَا أَرْسَلْنَا فِي قَرْيَةٍ مِنْ نَبِيٍّ إِلَّا أَخَذْنَا أَهْلَهَا بِالْبَأْسَاءِ وَالضَّرَّاءِ لَعَلَّهُمْ يَضَّرَّعُونَ ﴿٩٤﴾

When we feel "safe" on the shore, many of us become complacent. We don't see our "need" of God. We become arrogant and drunk with the illusion of "self-sufficiency". So sometimes out of His mercy, Allah pulls us to Him through storms. Because the duaa that we make while "comfortable" on the shore is not like the duaa we make while in the middle of the ocean in a storm.

When we study the lives of those nearest to Allah, we find that they all went through storms, and that every single one of them only survived those storms by humbling themselves and turning to Allah. Yunus (AS) in the belly of the fish. Muhammad (pbuh) after the death of his wife and the abuse at Taif. Ayoub (AS) at the peak of sickness and loss. Yaqoob (AS) when he lost two of his sons. Musa (AS) when he accidentally killed a man and is running for his life.

Study the duas of every single one of them. They are all the same. Humility and need. And hope in Allah. Total reliance on Allah. Not depending on themselves or anything else. Not thinking "they got this". Total tawheed and humility.

Yunus (AS):

"And [mention] the man of the fish, when he went off in anger and thought that We would not decree [anything] upon him. And he called out within the darkness's, 'There is no deity except You; exalted are You. Indeed, I have been one of the wrongdoers.'" (Quran 21:87)

وَذَا النُّونِ إِذْ ذَهَبَ مُغَاضِبًا فَظَنَّ أَنْ لَنْ نَقْدِرَ عَلَيْهِ فَنَادَى فِي الظُّلُمَاتِ أَنْ لَا إِلَهَ إِلَّا أَنْتَ سُبْحَانَكَ إِنِّي كُنْتُ مِنَ الظَّالِمِينَ ۝

The Prophet Muhammad (pbuh) said, regarding this duaa of Yunus (AS): "No Muslim person says it, for any situation whatsoever, except that Allah Most High answers his call." (Tirmidhi)

Muhammad (pbuh) at Taif:

"To You, my Lord, I complain of my weakness, lack of support and the humiliation I am made to receive. Most Compassionate and Merciful! You are the Lord of the weak, and you are my Lord. To whom do You leave me? To a distant person who receives me with hostility? Or to an enemy You have given power over me? As long as you are not displeased with me, I do not care what I face. I would, however, be much happier with Your mercy. I seek refuge in the light of Your face by which all darkness is dispelled and all matters in the heavens and hearth are set right against incurring your wrath or being the subject of your anger. To You I submit, until I earn Your pleasure. Everything is powerless without your support."

Ayoub (AS):

"And [mention] Job, when he called to his Lord, 'Indeed, adversity has touched me, and you are the Most Merciful of the merciful.'" (Quran 21:83)

وَأَيُّوبَ إِذْ نَادَى رَبَّهُ أَنِّي مَسَّنِيَ الضُّرُّ وَأَنْتَ أَرْحَمُ الرَّاحِمِينَ ٨٣

Yaqoob (AS):

"He said, 'I make complaint of my anguish and my sorrow unto God; I know from God what you do not know.'" (Quran 12:86)

قَالَ إِنَّمَا أَشْكُو بَثِّي وَحُزْنِي إِلَى اللَّهِ وَأَعْلَمُ مِنَ اللَّهِ مَا لَا تَعْلَمُونَ ٨٦

Musa (AS):

"So he watered [their flocks] for them; then he went back to the shade and said, 'My Lord, indeed I am, for whatever good You would send down to me, in need.'" (Quran 28:24)

فَسَقَى لَهُمَا ثُمَّ تَوَلَّى إِلَى الظِّلِّ فَقَالَ رَبِّ إِنِّي لِمَا أَنْزَلْتَ إِلَيَّ مِنْ خَيْرٍ فَقِيرٌ ٢٤

Every single one of them complained *to* Allah. They never complained *about* Allah. And they all turned to Allah in humility and hope.

The following duaas are some prophetically prescribed supplications for those going through difficulty:

DUAA 1: RELIEF FROM HARDSHIPS

"There is none worthy of worship but Allah the Mighty, the Forbearing. There is none worthy of worship but Allah, Lord of the Magnificent Throne. There is none worthy of worship but Allah, Lord of the heavens and Lord of the earth, and Lord of the Noble Throne." (Sahih Bukhari 8:154).

لَا إِلَهَ إِلَّا اللهُ الْعَظِيمُ الْحَلِيمُ لَا إِلَهَ إِلَّا اللهُ رَبُّ الْعَرْشِ الْعَظِيمِ لَا إِلَهَ إِلَّا اللهُ رَبُّ السَّمَوَاتِ وَرَبُّ الْأَرْضِ وَرَبُّ الْعَرْشِ الْكَرِيمِ

DUAA 2: TO RECTIFY ALL YOUR AFFAIRS

"O Allah, I hope for Your mercy. Do not leave me to myself even for the blink of an eye. Rectify all of my affairs for me. There is none worthy of worship but You."
(Sunan Abi Dawud 5090)

اللَّهُمَّ رَحْمَتَكَ أَرْجُو فَلَا تَكِلْنِي إِلَى نَفْسِي طَرْفَةَ عَيْنٍ وَأَصْلِحْ لِي شَأْنِي كُلَّهُ لَا إِلَهَ إِلَّا أَنْتَ

DUAA 3: SAFETY FROM SHIRK

"Allah, Allah is my Lord. I do not associate anything with Him (shirk)." (Sunan Abi Dawud 1525)

اللهُ اللهُ رَبِّي لا أُشْرِكُ به شيئًا

DUAA 4: DUAA FOR EASE

"Oh Allah, nothing is easy, except what you make easy. And, if You will, You make what is difficult easy." (Ibn Hibban 2427)

اللَّهُمَّ لَا سَهْلَ إِلاَّ مَا جَعَلْتَهُ سَهْلاً وأَنْتَ تَجْعَلُ الْحَزْنَ إِذَا شِئْتَ سَهْلاً

DUAA 5: ALLAH DOES AS HE WILLS

"It is the Decree of Allah and He does whatever He wills." (Sahih Muslim 2664)

قَدَرُ اللَّهِ وَمَا شَاءَ فَعَلَ

DUAA 6: FOR GRIEF AND ANXIETY

The Prophet (*pbuh*) said, "No person suffers any anxiety or grief, and says (this duaa), except that Allah removes his distress and grief and replaces it with joy.":

اللَّهُمَّ إِنِّى عَبْدُكَ ابْنُ عَبْدِكَ ابْنُ أَمَتِكَ نَاصِيَتِى بِيَدِكَ مَاضٍ فِيَّ حُكْمُكَ عَدْلٌ فِيَّ قَضَاؤُكَ أَسْأَلُكَ بِكُلِّ اسْمٍ هُوَ لَكَ سَمَّيْتَ بِهِ نَفْسَكَ أَوْ أَنْزَلْتَهُ فِى كِتَابِكَ أَوْ عَلَّمْتَهُ أَحَدًا مِنْ خَلْقِكَ أَوِ اسْتَأْثَرْتَ بِهِ فِى عِلْمِ الْغَيْبِ عِنْدَكَ أَنْ تَجْعَلَ الْقُرْآنَ رَبِيعَ قَلْبِى وَنُورَ صَدْرِى وجَلَاءَ حُزْنِى وذَهَابَ هَمِّى

"O Allah, I am Your slave, son of Your slave, son of Your female slave, my forelock is in Your hand, Your Command over me is forever executed and Your Decree over me is Just. I ask You by every Name Belonging to You which You Named Yourself with, or Revealed in Your Book, or You Taught to any of Your Creation, or You have Preserved in the knowledge of the unseen with You, that You Make the Qur'an the life of my heart and the light of my breast, and a departure for my sorrow and a release for my anxiety." (Musnad of Imam Ahmad 3528)

DUAA 7: THERE'S NO CHANGE OR POWER WITHOUT ALLAH

"There is no change in state and no power, except by Allah."

لا حَوْلَ وَلا قُوَّةَ إِلا بِالله

The Messenger of Allah (pbuh) said: "For the person who reads 'La hawla wa la quwwata illa billah', it is a cure for 99 diseases. The mildest of which is grief." (Sunan Ibn Majah 3825)

DUAA 8: SHOWING THANKS FOR SAFETY FROM CALAMITY

Sometimes it is not our own difficulties we are witnessing, but rather the difficulties of others around us. When seeing others going through difficulties, we must be thankful to Allah for saving us from a similar situation. The following should be recited when seeing others in difficulties. We should also pray for the person so that he/she is relieved from the problem:

"Praise is to Allah Who has spared me what He has afflicted you with, and preferred me greatly above much of what He has created." (Jami al Tirmidhi 3431)

الْحَمْدُ لِلهِ الذِي عَافَانِي مِمَّا ابْتلاكَ بِه و فَضَّلَنِي على كَثِيرٍ مِمَّنْ خَلق تَفْضِيلًا

DUAA 9: AAFIYAH

Al-Abbas (RA), the uncle of the Prophet Muhammed (pbuh) came to the Prophet (pbuh) and said: "Oh messenger of Allah, teach me a Duaa." The Prophet (pbuh) said: "Oh my uncle, say:

'Allahumma inni as'aluka al Aafiyah'.
'Oh Allah, I ask you for Aafiyah.'"

اللّهُمّ إِنِّي أَسْأَلُكَ الْعَافِيَةَ

Al-Abbas (R.A.) later came back and said: "Oh messenger of Allah (pbuh), this duaa seems a little short. I want something big." The Prophet Muhammed (pbuh) said: "My dear uncle, ask Allah for Aafiyah for Wallahi (by Allah), you cannot be given anything better than Aafiyah." (Riyadh As Saliheen, Sunan At-Tirmidhi).

Aafiyah includes: having ease, being saved from afflictions, being healthy, having enough money, having your children protected, being forgiven and not punished, etc. So with this duaa, you are essentially asking:

"Oh Allah, protect me from pain and suffering in this life and the next."

"Oh Allah, I ask You to save me from distress, grief, hardship, harm, and tests, etc."

All of the above and much more are included in this comprehensive duaa prescribed by the Prophet (pbuh).

DUAA 10: LOSS OF A LOVED ONE

The Prophet (pbuh) said: "Allah says, 'I have nothing to give but Paradise as a reward to my slave, who if I cause his dear friend (or relative) to die, remains patient (and hopes for Allah's Reward).'" [Al-Bukhari]

One of the hardest tests in this life is the loss of a child. The Messenger of Allah (pbuh) said:

"When a person's child dies, Allah says to His angels, 'You have taken the child of My slave.'

They say, 'Yes.'

He says, 'You have taken the apple of his eye.'

They say, 'Yes.'

He says, 'What did My slave say?'

They say, 'He praised you and said "Innaa lillaahi wa inna ilayhi raaji'oon (Verily to Allah we belong and unto Him is our return).'

Allah says, 'Build for My slave a house in Paradise and call it the house of praise.'" (Al-Tirmidhi 942, Classed as hasn by-al-Albaani in al-Silsilah al-Saheehah 1408)

The Prophet (pbuh) also said:

"Their little ones are the little ones (da'amees) of Paradise. When one of them meets his father (or his parents) he takes hold of his garment (or his hand) as I am taking told of the hem of your garment, and he does not let go until Allah admits him and his father (or parent) to Paradise." (Narrated by Muslim 2635)

Umm Salamah (RA) reported: "I heard the Messenger of Allah (pbuh) say, "When a person suffers from a calamity and utters:

Inna lillahi wa inna ilaihi raji`un. Allahumma ujurni fi musibati, wakhluf li khairan minha. 'We belong to Allah and to Him we shall return. O Allah! Compensate me in my affliction, recompense my loss and give me something better in exchange for it,' then Allah surely compensates him with reward and a better substitute.'" *(Sahih Muslim)*

إِنّا لله وَإِنّا إِلَـيْهِ راجِعـون اللهُـمّ أُجُـرْنى فى مُصِـيبَتى وَاخْلُـفْ لى خَيْـراً مِنْها

When Umm Salamah's (RA) husband died, she repeated this duaa as taught by the Prophet (pbuh). She later married to the Prophet (pbuh) himself.

It is important to understand that "what is better" may come in many forms. It does not mean that when we lose a spouse or child, we are going to get a "replacement", or that we are going to get a better spouse or child. Allah can give us "better than it" in whatever form He wills. Sometimes it is in the hereafter. Sometimes it is in elevation of our status with Allah or in the nearness to Him. This is the formula that was prescribed by the Prophet (pbuh) for a woman who was grieving the loss of her husband. But, this duaa is a prescription for any loss. When we say this duaa in our loss, Allah will reward us and will give us what is better in some form.

Tool 7: Make Allah Your Focus

This is one of the most essential elements of spiritual health and happiness. As humans, we can only "look" in one direction at any given time. What our heart is "looking at" in any given moment becomes our greatest concern–at the expense of all other concerns. When the object of our focus is the creation–what they think, what they are going to say or do–we suffer greatly. We become slaves. And then we act in oppressive ways as a result. But the first person we end up oppressing is ourselves. When we become slaves to the opinions of others, we enslaves ourselves to them.

I have had cases of families who send their own daughters back to abusive homes, out of fear of "what people will say" if she gets divorced. This is slavery. And oppression of self and others. When the way in which we act or don't act is dictated by other people's assessments and judgements, we are worshiping the opinions of others. And there is nothing more oppressive than worshiping something as fickle and baseless as the assessments of others. One day, they will approve of you; the next day, they will disapprove. One day, something will be "in fashion" or "politically correct", and the next day it will be the opposite. Attaching ourselves to the opinions of others is like chaining ourselves to the back of a car with a blind driver; we only get dragged around. And destroyed.

When we initiate a fundamental internal shift and make Allah the Focal point, we release those chains. We become free to act as God said we *should*, rather than the way that is dictated by fear of social judgment. That's where true courage and moral strength comes from. It requires a fundamental detachment (from anything else) and then reattachment (to God alone). This is the essence of "*la illah illa Allah*" (kalima). It means that your ultimate focal point and Director is not the people, it is not culture or fashion or fame. It is Allah and Allah alone. Even the linguistic structure of the kalima is transformative. It begins with a total negation: "la illaha": "there is nothing worthy of being at the very center". First, it clears the slate completely. And then it introduces the One and only True Illah (object of ultimate focus, worship, and obedience): Allah. God. That's it. Nothing else. Not money. Not people. Not political correctness. Not fame. Not fashion. Not power. Not another person. And not our own selves and desires.

See, we all have desires. We all have inclinations. And those desires and inclinations may or may not be in line with the laws of God. As believers, we realize that the very essence of *Islam* is submission. As Muslims, we have wholeheartedly chosen to submit to God and His prescription for life. We wholeheartedly have chosen to worship God—not our desires or inclinations. This means when our desires or inclinations go against a commandment of God, we struggle against the inclination—not the commandment. This is the essence of mujahadat ul nafs (struggle against lower self/ego). Without that higher struggle, we become slaves to every desire and command of our lower self.

For example, what happens when a person has a desire to drink alcohol? What happens when a person has a desire for someone who is not their spouse? Does the *desire itself* make it moral to drink alcohol or commit adultery? Of course not. We are not held accountable for the *desire itself*. We all have desires. But, we *are* held accountable for what we *do* with our desires. Who is in command? My desire or God? Do we give into the desire and allow it to command our behavior? Or do we struggle against the desire for the sake of Allah? And if we do struggle against a desire for the sake of God, we are actually rewarded for that very struggle. It is just like the reward given to the person who struggles against their desire to get drunk or high. And it is like the one who has a desire for someone who isn't their spouse gets rewarded for resisting adultery. *Desire doesn't define morality.* And ironically no one judges a person who simply believes that alcohol or adultery (zina) is immoral. No one calls them an "alcoho-phobe" or "zina-phobe". Even if others disagree with our beliefs, people are still "allowed" to believe alcohol and adultery are immoral without being "ostracized" and *forced* into "compliance".

THE NEW AGE RELIGION

But the "new age religion" of today is *not* tolerant. It commands you to worship yourself, your "hawa": Your desires. Your opinions. Your inclinations. Your orientation. And those desires, opinions, inclinations, orientations become your ultimate guiding force. Not a higher morality. Not God. Not scripture. The ultimate law and code is your own desires, your own definitions. The *hawa* becomes the *illah*. This is what Allah speaks about in the Quran when He says:

"Have you seen the one who has taken his own desires as his god? And Allah has let him go astray, despite having knowledge and has set a seal upon his hearing and his heart, and put over his vision a veil. So who will guide him after Allah? Then will you not be reminded?" (Quran 45:23)

أَفَرَأَيْتَ مَنِ اتَّخَذَ إِلَهَهُ
هَوَاهُ وَأَضَلَّهُ اللَّهُ عَلَى عِلْمٍ
وَخَتَمَ عَلَى سَمْعِهِ وَقَلْبِهِ
وَجَعَلَ عَلَى بَصَرِهِ غِشَاوَةً
فَمَنْ يَهْدِيهِ مِنْ بَعْدِ اللَّهِ
أَفَلَا تَذَكَّرُونَ ٢

And in this "new age religion", no one is allowed to "disbelieve". See, in Islam we are taught "there is no compulsion in religion/way of life" (Quran 2:256). We are told to say, "to you is your way and to us, is ours" (Quran 109:6). But not in this *new age religion*. There is no freedom. There is no tolerance. There *is* compulsion. You *must* believe. You *must* agree. And if you don't, you will be targeted in every possible way: in the court of public opinion, in your job, and in your credibility. Until you comply. You are *forced* to sign off on the beliefs of this *new age religion*. And you don't even have the right to teach your children something different. The "daees" (propagators) of this "new age religion" will come into your children's schools, change the curriculum, and force them to believe the only creed that is "allowed". And they will start as young as kindergarten to *force* allegiance to their beliefs. Nothing else is tolerated. And then the media will become the center of the proselytization mission. The new age "daawa" of Netflix will confuse your children until they are convinced that anyone who dares to believe otherwise is the "intolerant" "phobe". An entire section of the Quran will need to be reinterpreted and rewritten because it doesn't fit the compulsory "new age religion".

Deep water, we've entered. And our children are drowning in it.

The only true antidote to this mass confusion is making Allah the focus. Not society. Not political correctness. Not culture. Not fashion. Not other people's opinions and judgements. And not our own desires. Only one *Illah*. And that is God. Alone.

RESCUE FROM DESPAIR

The focus on Allah can free us and save us from deep confusion, but it can also rescue us from despair. One of the most toxic responses we can have to any difficulty in our life is to assume the worst about Allah. To believe that Allah "hates you" or is giving you that hardship because He is "angry with you" will poison your heart and rob you of your strength. But what about cases where someone has actually done something wrong? What if you actually have made a mistake–even a huge mistake. Can't the hardship actually be a consequence of a sin?

The answer is yes. Sometimes we face difficulties because of what our own hands have brought. But even in that case, it can be a mercy. Take the example of a loving parent. What happens when the child they love does something wrong–something self-sabotaging? What does a loving parent do? Well, if the parent didn't care about the ultimate well-being of the child, the parent might do nothing at all. But if the parent truly cared for the child, they would set up a consequence for that child. But what would be the purpose of that consequence? Would a loving parent set up consequences to hurt the child or because they "hated" the child? Or does the parent act out of mercy, to *teach* and *raise* the child (*tarbiyah*)? The consequences provided by a loving parent are in fact meant to protect the child from future, more severe consequences. So even if the child "deserved" that consequence, what do we call what the parent is doing?

We call it mercy.

Allah says:

"And indeed We will make them taste of the Penalty of this (life) prior to the supreme Penalty, in order that they may return (and repent)." (Quran 32:21)

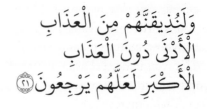

Even in cases where we actually "mess up", we should never think negatively about Allah or what He is doing. Allah is giving—even when He takes. He is purifying, even when He is testing. He is strengthening, even when he is trying us. He wants what is good for the believer. Always and infinitely more than a mother for her own child.

The Prophet (pbuh) said: "By Him in whose hand is my soul, if you did not sin, Allah would replace you with people who would sin and they would seek the forgiveness of Allah and He would forgive them." [Sahih Muslim]

SHIFTS THE FOCUS AWAY FROM OURSELVES

Even when we do make a mistake, we need to shift the focus away from ourselves. Often when we mess up, we end up focusing on the mistake, on the mess that we "caused". We focus on all the things we did wrong and all the terrible consequences. We focus on our own weakness and feelings of worthlessness. But we need to shift the focus away from ourselves completely. Shift the focus from your own weakness to Allah's strength. Shift the focus from your mistake to Allah's infinite mercy and forgiveness. When you do that, you move from constriction to expansion, and from paralysis to movement and growth.

We are all flawed. It's the design. But we are not meant to obsess over our own flaws. This is our humanness. We are meant to see those flaws so we can fix them. But the fixation should not be on ourselves, our faults, our weaknesses. The fixation should be on Allah. His mercy. His forgiveness. His strength. Only then will we grow through our mistakes, rather than getting lost in them. Only then will we be able to turn weakness into strength.

Only then will we be able to turn Shaytan's weapon against him. Shaytan wants to make you see only your shortcomings and mistakes so you feel hopeless, powerless and weak. He wants you to get stuck in your weaknesses, so you won't move. And so you won't repent or try again. But you have a Lord whose mercy encompasses all things (Quran 7:156).

Do you believe that all your weaknesses put together are greater than God's strength? Do you believe that all your sins put together are greater than Allah's mercy and forgiveness? And if you do, then you need to get to know who Allah really is.

Allah says:

"Say, O My servants who have transgressed against themselves [by sinning], do not despair of the mercy of Allah. Indeed, Allah forgives all sins. Indeed, it is He who is the Forgiving, the Merciful." (Quran 39:53)

قُلْ يَا عِبَادِيَ الَّذِينَ أَسْرَفُوا عَلَى أَنْفُسِهِمْ لَا تَقْنَطُوا مِنْ رَحْمَةِ اللَّهِ إِنَّ اللَّهَ يَغْفِرُ الذُّنُوبَ جَمِيعًا إِنَّهُ هُوَ الْغَفُورُ الرَّحِيمُ ۝

In the hadith Qudsi (34) Allah tells us:

عَنْ أَنَسٍ رَضِيَ اللهُ عَنْهُ قَالَ سَمِعْتُ رَسُولَ اللهِ صَلَّى الله عَلَيْهِ وَ سَلَّمَ يَقُولُ قَالَ اللهُ تَعَالَى يَا ابْنَ ادَمَ إِنَّكَ مَا دَعَوْتَنِي وَرَجَوْتَنِي غَفَرْتُ لَكَ عَلَى مَا كَانَ مِنْكَ وَلَا أُبَالِي يَا ابْنَ ادَمَ لَوْ بَلَغَتْ ذُنُوبُكَ عَنَانَ السَّماءِ ثُمَّ اسْتَغْفَرْتَنِي غَفَرْتُ لَكَ يَا ابْنَ ادَمَ إِنَّكَ لَوْ أَتَيْتَنِي بِقُرَابِ الْأَرْضِ خَطَايا ثُمَّ لَقِيتَنِي لَا تُشْرِكُ بِي شَيْئاً لَأَتَيْتُكَ بِقُرَابِها مَغْفِرَةً رواهُ الترمذى وكذلك أحمد وسنده حسن

The Prophet (pbuh) said that Allah said: "O son of Adam, so long as you call upon Me and ask of Me, I shall forgive you for what you have done, and I shall not mind. O son of Adam, were your sins to reach the clouds of the sky and were you then to ask forgiveness of Me, I would forgive you. O son of Adam, were you to come to Me with sins nearly as great as the earth and were you then to face Me, ascribing no partner to Me, I would bring you forgiveness nearly as great as it." (Tirmidhi and Ahmad)

Making God our focus is the most powerful way to free the heart from despair and from the chains that bind us in this life. The most powerful way to transform our reaction to any of our life events, is to see through them. Not to get lost in the hologram or the illusion of pain or pleasure. To see who it all came from. When you see the Most Merciful as the Sender, it will soften your heart and extract acceptance and even contentment.

Tool 8: Clean the Heart

Keeping the heart clean is essential to spiritual and emotional health. But many things end up cluttering and staining the heart. For this reason, consistent cleansing of the heart is necessary.

ISTIGHFAAR

One essential way to clean and heal the heart is through istighfaar (repentance). The Prophet (pbuh) said: "Whoever does a lot of Istighfar (asking for forgiveness), Allah will provide him a way out of each concern he has, and will solve all his troubles, and will provide him with livelihood from sources that were not known to him." (Ahmad)

When the heart is consistently cleaned from the stain of sin, it can function in a healthy way. The heart is a lens. If that lens is dirty, it will see the world in a distorted way. It will see the world as dark and will not be able to understand right from wrong. When the lens is foggy, the vision is foggy. We must clean the lens so that our inner sight (baseera) can be clear. And sharp.

Allah says:

"So have they not traveled through the earth and have hearts by which to reason and ears by which to hear? For indeed, it is not the eyes that are blinded, but blinded are the hearts which are within the breasts." (Quran 22:46)

أَفَلَمْ يَسِيرُوا فِي الْأَرْضِ فَتَكُونَ لَهُمْ قُلُوبٌ يَعْقِلُونَ بِهَا أَوْ آذَانٌ يَسْمَعُونَ بِهَا فَإِنَّهَا لَا تَعْمَى الْأَبْصَارُ وَلَكِنْ تَعْمَى الْقُلُوبُ الَّتِي فِي الصُّدُورِ ﴿٤٦﴾

LET GO OF GRUDGES

The heart is also the place where we connect to Allah. If the heart is not clean, our connection to Allah will be harmed. When the heart is full of rancor and grudges, it takes up space that is necessary to connect to Allah. Also, when we hold onto a grudge, we end up giving too much power to another person and end up making something other than Allah our primary focus. The most powerful way to let go of grudges is to "let go and let God". Find peace in knowing that Allah sees all and that Allah is the Most Just. Find peace in knowing that God will give you justice. So clear your heart and don't give away space inside you to those who have hurt you.

Tool 9: The Remembrance of God

We can only find shelter in our emotional storms by turning to God. We can only find security in Him, when everything else around us is unstable. Salvation is to find certainty in God's promise, when our lives are full of uncertainty. Find shelter in the remembrance of Allah. In the remembrance of Allah (thikr) is a healing for all that is in the hearts. And it is in the remembrance of Allah that the hearts find true joy. When Allah revealed the prescription for salah and its specific timings, He ended the ayah by saying this was how we would find joy and internal satisfaction:

"So be patient over what they say and exalt [Allah] with praise of your Lord before the rising of the sun and before its setting; and during periods of the night [exalt Him] and at the ends of the day, that you may have (spiritual) joy." (Quran 20:130)

فَاصْبِرْ عَلَى مَا يَقُولُونَ وَسَبِّحْ بِحَمْدِ رَبِّكَ قَبْلَ طُلُوعِ الشَّمْسِ وَقَبْلَ غُرُوبِهَا وَمِنْ آنَاءِ اللَّيْلِ فَسَبِّحْ وَأَطْرَافَ النَّهَارِ لَعَلَّكَ تَرْضَى ﴿١٣٠﴾

The remembrance of Allah is what gives us life. The Prophet (pubh) said:

"The example of the one who remembers his Lord and the one who does not, is like the living and the dead." (Sahih al-Bukhari 6407)

مَثَلُ الَّذِى يَذْكُرُ رَبَّهُ وَالَّذِى لاَ يَذْكُرُ مَثَلُ الْحَيِّ وَالْمَيِّتِ

The Prophet (pbuh) also said:

"The parable of the house in which Allah is remembered, and the house in which Allah is not remembered, is that of the living and the dead." (Sahīh Muslim 779)

مَثَلُ الْبَيْتِ الَّذِى يَذْكَرُ اللَّه فِيهِ وَالْبَيْتِ الَّذِى لَا يُذْكَرُ اللَّه فِيهِ مَثَلُ الْحَيِّ وَالْمَيِّتِ

The Prophet (pbuh) told us that when we remember God, God remembers us.

He (pbuh) said: "Allah says, 'I treat My servant as he hopes that I would treat him. I am with him whenever he remembers Me: if he thinks of Me, I think of him; if he mentions Me in company, I mention him in an even better company. If he draws near to Me a hand's span, I draw near to him an arm's length; and if he draws near to Me an arm's length, I draw closer by a distance of two outstretched arms nearer to him; and if he comes to Me walking, I go to him running.'" (Al-Bukhari and Muslim)

And those who turn away from the remembrance of God, end up suffering in this life before the next. Allah warns us:

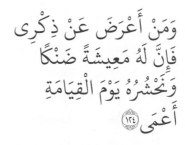

"And whoever turns away from My remembrance, indeed for him will be a narrow (miserable) life, and We will gather him on the Day of Resurrection blind." (Quran 20:124)

The remembrance of Allah provides both healing and protection. Everyday should include a *consistent* prescription of thikr (remembrance of Allah). The following is an essential 3-part *daily* thikr prescription:

1. SALAH

The prescribed 5 daily prayers are the oxygen of our hearts. If we stop praying, we stop breathing. Just as our physical heart cannot function without oxygen, our spiritual heart cannot function without thikr, specifically salah. And the medicine of salah is given by the Creator at specified times for a reason. Just like a prescription of medicine given by a doctor, we must follow the prescription at its appointed times because the Doctor knows what He is doing. God is high above any analogy and is Greater than any doctor. When He prescribes fajr to be *before* the sun rises, it's because *He knows what He is doing.* What would happen if we took lifesaving medicine prescribed by a doctor and skipped doses every day? What would happen if we took all 5 doses before we sleep? We know that medicine must be taken as it was prescribed and at the time it was prescribed to keep us alive and healthy.

Salah is the oxygen of the heart. It keeps us alive. And yet we often make excuses about prayer. But can you imagine saying "I'm busy right now at work, so I'll breathe tonight" or "I'm at the mall or the airport, so I'll breathe after I get home". We don't compromise about oxygen because we know it's keeping us alive. Know that salah is keeping you alive. There is no other way to put it.

Despite this Reality, for many people, the needs of the soul are secondary to the needs of the body. We would go to any length to "answer the calls of nature" if we need to use the bathroom. We will walk out of meetings, exams, class, or work to use the bathroom. We will wake from sleep at four in the morning or pull our car over in the middle of a journey, to use the bathroom. But, often we would not do any of this to pray? In Ramadan, if we miss fajr, we are devastated. As soon as we wake and see the sun, we panic. Why? Because we missed suhoor (pre-dawn meal). So for one month out of the year, missing Fajr is a tragedy. But what happens for the other 11 months of the year when we oversleep and miss fajr? We grieve over one missed meal for the stomach, while we are unflinched that our soul is starving.

Salah is also the first thing we will be asked about on the Day of Judgement. The Prophet (pbuh) said: "The first thing for which a person will be brought to account on the Day of Judgement will be his Salat. If it is found to be complete, then it will be recorded as complete and if anything is lacking, He will say, 'Look and see if you can find any voluntary prayers with which to complete what he neglected of his obligatory prayers.' Then the rest of his deeds will be reckoned in like manner." (Sunan al-Nasai, Kitab al-Salat, Hadith 466)

In the Quran, Allah describes a deep part of human nature. He says:

"Indeed, mankind was created anxious (and impatient). When evil afflicts him, he panics. And when good touches him, he is withholding [of it]." (Quran 70:19-21)	إِنَّ الْإِنْسَانَ خُلِقَ هَلُوعًا ﴿١٩﴾ إِذَا مَسَّهُ الشَّرُّ جَزُوعًا ﴿٢٠﴾ وَإِذَا مَسَّهُ الْخَيْرُ مَنُوعًا ﴿٢١﴾

But after stating this truth about human nature, Allah tells us the exception. He teaches us that there is one group of people who are able to rise above this basic nature. There is one group who does not panic when faced with difficulty and does not become stingy when given blessings.

Allah says:

> *"Except the observers of prayer—*
> *those who are constant in their*
> *prayer." (Quran 70:22-23)*

إِلَّا الْمُصَلِّينَ ۝ الَّذِينَ هُمْ
عَلَى صَلَاتِهِمْ دَائِمُونَ ۝

Prayer itself becomes a buffer from panicking and withholding. When Allah spoke to Musa (AS), the first commandment He gave was to establish prayer for God's remembrance. Allah proclaimed:

> *"And I have chosen you, so listen to*
> *what is revealed [to you]. Indeed,*
> *I am God. There is no deity except*
> *Me, so worship Me and establish*
> *prayer for My remembrance."*
> *(Quran 20:13-14)*

وَأَنَا اخْتَرْتُكَ فَاسْتَمِعْ لِمَا
يُوحَى ۝ إِنَّنِي أَنَا اللَّهُ لَا
إِلَهَ إِلَّا أَنَا فَاعْبُدْنِي وَأَقِمِ
الصَّلَاةَ لِذِكْرِى ۝

We are not only commanded to pray; we are commanded to *establish* prayer in our lives. This means we do not just pray when it's convenient or only when we "feel like it". Prayer is not something we *sometimes* do. Prayer is not something we do only in Ramadan or during big rituals or holidays. It is not something we do only when we are happy, or only when we are desperate and we need something. It is not something we do only when we are on a "spiritual high", but then stop praying when we "don't feel it anymore". *Establishing* prayer means it's a constant. A non-negotiable in our lives. Like oxygen. Like breathing. We breathe when we are up and we breathe when we are down. We breathe when we get what we want and we breathe when we don't get what we want. We breathe when we are free and we breathe when we are busy. We breathe to stay alive. And that's not negotiable. That is what "*establishing* salah" means.

And when we do that, when we truly establish salah in our lives, we are given a special strength. Salah is a shield from harm, a shield from shaytan and from our own lower selves (nafs). It is a deterrent against sin. It is a purification.

But salah also gives us a special resilience. While the default of human nature is to panic and fall apart during hardships, the one who establishes salah does not. The one who establishes salah is gifted with a God-given resilience in the face of challenges and tests. It is the spiritual immune system. Those who remember Allah during times of ease, Allah will keep their feet firm during times of hardship. Allah said, "O you who have believed, if you support Allah, He will support you and plant your feet firmly." (Quran 47:8)

2. ATHKAR

The Prophet (pbuh) taught us about the deep importance of remembering Allah throughout our day. He (pbuh) has taught us a supplication (duaa) for every part of life, from the mundane to the sacred. It is essential that we maintain a consistent regiment of athkar (daily remembrance) that we say consistently.

One of the times when it is essential to have a regiment of athkar is in the morning after Fajr prayer. These are called *athkar al-sabaah* (morning remembrance). This practice guides us and protects us for the rest of the day. It becomes a shield (hisn), hence the famous duaa collection was titled: Hisnul Muslim (The Fortress of a Muslim). And that is exactly what our athkar do for us. They protect us. They change our mindset and our lives.

The second time it is essential to read our athkar is in the evening after Asr prayer. This practice protects us until the next morning. And the third time it is emphasized to read our athkar is before we sleep. This practice protects us while we sleep. Besides these 3 essential times, there are short athkar that the Prophet (pbuh) would say throughout his day. He taught us duaas for leaving the house, before eating, after eating, during travel, and even before intimacy. The more we can incorporate this practice (sunnah) into our everyday lives, the more peace we will find in our lives and the stronger our hearts will become.

There are many Apps for duaas that allow us to have access to the supplications that we don't have memorized. It is also important to remember that even a little amount of athkar, done consistently, will have a massive effect on one's life and state of mind. A small amount done consistently is better than a huge amount, done inconsistently. For example, if you do 1,500 sit ups one day, it will have less impact than doing just 50 sit ups every day, for a month.

Allah loves the actions that are *consistent*–even if they are small.

Aisha (RA) said: "Once the Prophet came while a woman was sitting with me." He said, "Who is she?" I replied, "She is so and so," and told him about her (excessive) praying. He said disapprovingly, "Do (good) deeds which is within your capacity (without being overtaxed) as Allah does not get tired (of giving rewards) but (surely) you will get tired. And the best deed (act of Worship) in the sight of Allah is that which is done regularly." (Sahih Bukhari, Hadith 42)

3. QURAN

It is necessary for us to have a consistent, daily relationship with the book of Allah. The Quran is in and of itself a healing for the diseases that afflict our hearts.
Allah says:

"O mankind, there has to come to you instruction from your Lord and healing for what is in the chests and guidance and mercy for the believers. Say, 'In the bounty of Allah and in His mercy - in that let them rejoice; it is better than what they accumulate.'"
(Quran 10:57-58)

يَا أَيُّهَا النَّاسُ قَدْ جَاءَتْكُمْ مَوْعِظَةٌ مِنْ رَبِّكُمْ وَشِفَاءٌ لِمَا فِي الصُّدُورِ وَهُدًى وَرَحْمَةٌ لِلْمُؤْمِنِينَ ۝ قُلْ بِفَضْلِ اللَّهِ وَبِرَحْمَتِهِ فَبِذَلِكَ فَلْيَفْرَحُوا هُوَ خَيْرٌ مِمَّا يَجْمَعُونَ ۝

The relationship with the Quran should be one of transformation, not just recitation or decoration. Many of us have a very distant relationship with the Quran. For some people that relationship is just ritualistic. The goal becomes just to "finish" the Quran. Often, the Quran is only recited in Ramadan, but very little outside of that. Sometimes, even if the Quran is recited regularly–or even memorized–there is no understanding of what it is actually saying to us. Many people invest years into teaching their children to read and memorize the Quran, but there is no comprehension of its meaning.

Sometimes the Quran is just used for decoration on beautiful plaques with beautiful calligraphy, or it is placed on necklaces for "protection". Sometimes it is only recited when someone dies. But the Quran was revealed to *transform* us. And its words are just as relevant today, as they were 1400 years ago. If you take a sincere step towards understanding the book of Allah, you will find yourself in it. You will find your own story. The Quran will start to speak to you. To *your* pain. To *your* struggle. But you must take that first step.

Tool 10: Take Action

There are two types of actions: Actions of the heart and actions of the limbs.

When Musa (AS) stood at the Red Sea, Pharoah and his army approached. He looked trapped. His people started to despair. But Musa (AS) saw through the illusion, and focused his heart on only one thing: Allah. *The focused vision of his heart allowed his feet to remain firmly planted at the peak of his trial.*

Allah says: "When the two groups came face to face, the companions of Moses cried out, 'We are overtaken for sure.' Moses reassured [them]: "Absolutely not! My Lord is certainly with me–He will guide me through." (Quran 26:61-62)

Musa (AS) had total conviction and trust in Allah, but he also did not stand passively. His heart took the internal action of tawakkul (trust), but Allah instructed him to also *take external action*:

"So We inspired Moses: 'Strike the sea with your staff', and the sea was split, each part was like a huge mountain." (Quran 26:63)

Both Hajar (AS) and Musa (AS) were saved by Allah *after they took external action*. It is, however, crucial to understand that salvation does not come *from* the action itself. Salvation does not come *from* our efforts. The sea did not split *by* the actions of Musa (AS). Water did not rise from the desert *by* the actions of Hajar (AS). Any one of us could strike an ocean with the largest stick we find; It won't split the sea. Any one of us could run seven times between hills. It won't make water come from the sand. But if we do not have the power to save ourselves or others, why are we commanded to take action? We are commanded to take action only because it is *part of our worship and obedience to God.*

The openings in our lives come *from God*. And God alone. The openings do not come from our hard work. Our efforts. Our tools or helpers. This Truth is part of our tawheed to understand. And internalize. And once we do internalize this Reality, it will remove the burdens we carry. This concept of Tawheed has the power to crumble even the most massive of mountains that we carry. Many of us cannot find peace and cannot sleep at night because we carry burdens that are not ours to carry. We carry the burdens of solving every problem, saving everyone we love, fixing everything that's broken around us. But we cannot. We cannot solve or fix or save. Anything.

Only God can.

So, we must put down the mountains we carry on our back. Let go of the soul-crushing burdens. We are not the savior. Especially for women, this false savior complex becomes a sort of unspoken covenant. The fear of "abandoning" someone who "needs" us, has kept many people hostage in abusive, toxic relationships, and environments. But this fear is based on a myth. The myth is that *we* can "save" the Narcissist or abuser. We believe we can "save" a drowning person who *does not want to be saved*. And so long as we believe these myths, we will continue to suffer. And in the end, we don't save the drowning person. We only drown along with them.

Consider the lesson Allah taught even His beloved, Prophet Muhammad (pbuh).

Allah says:

"Verily you cannot guide whom you love, but it is God who guides whom He wills [to be guided]; and He is fully aware of all who would let themselves be guided." (Quran 28:56)	إِنَّكَ لَا تَهْدِى مَنْ أَحْبَبْتَ وَلَكِنَّ اللَّهَ يَهْدِى مَنْ يَشَاءُ وَهُوَ أَعْلَمُ بِالْمُهْتَدِينَ ۝

Allah also says to the Prophet (pbuh):

"Perhaps you will torment yourself to death [with grief] because they refuse to believe." (Quran 26:3)	لَعَلَّكَ بَاخِعٌ نَفْسَكَ أَلَّا يَكُونُوا مُؤْمِنِينَ ۝

There is a very profound lesson in these verses. Prophet Muhammad (pbuh) was the best of creation. If even he did not have the power to save those he loved, how can we?

TAKING ACTION IS WORSHIP

Just as we must understand this reality as part of our tawheed, we must also understand that taking action is part of our ibaadah (worship). One day Prophet Muhammad (pbuh) noticed a Bedouin leaving his camel without tying it. He asked the Bedouin, "Why don't you tie down your camel?" The Bedouin answered, "I placed my trust in Allah." At that, the Prophet (pbuh) said, "Tie your camel and place your trust in Allah." (Tirmidhi)

When we are in pain, "tying our camel" means first digging deep. This process of discovery and introspection may require assistance and/or therapy. It is essential to know that there is absolutely no religious or spiritual shame in seeking help. In fact, that therapy itself can also be part of our worship (tying the camel). But this first step requires courage and truthfulness. It means being brave enough to take a real, honest look at ourselves and our lives. And then having the fortitude and tawakkul (trust in God) to take action. And that action must be with and by Allah. We must make sure to seek help and guidance from Allah throughout the process–before, during and after we "tie our camel". Throughout our journey.

Tool 11: Istikhara

Istikhara is a profound and necessary part of the believer's journey to Allah. The istikhara duaa begins by acknowledging a few essential Truths:

1. Allah's ability and our inability
2. Allah's knowledge and our lack of knowledge
3. Allah's knowledge of the unseen

This Reality is the very essence of istikhara.

Imagine there is a child driving a car, while blindfolded. This is analogous to you and I trying to steer the direction of our own lives, without guidance. We are unable to drive and we are blind to all of the unseen. We do not know the future or what is hidden in the minds, hearts and intentions of others. We do not know which direction, which choice or which person will bring us goodness and which will bring us harm. Therefore, we must not try to drive our own lives, as we are totally blindfolded. We must ask Allah to "drive". And that is what istikhara does. It is a duaa that begins by telling Allah that He is able, while we are *unable*. That He knows, while we do not know. And then we proceed to ask Him to *direct* the course of our affairs and to *direct* the outcome. We are not asking for a dream or a sign. We are asking Allah to take over the steering wheel.

HOW TO PERFORM ISTIKHARA

The Prophet (pbuh) said, "If anyone of you thinks of doing any job (or action), he should offer two Rakat of extra prayer and say (after the prayer)":

اللَّهُمَّ إِنِّي أَسْتَخِيرُكَ بِعِلْمِكَ وَأَسْتَقْدِرُكَ بِقُدْرَتِكَ وَأَسْأَلُكَ مِنْ فَضْلِكَ الْعَظِيمِ فَإِنَّكَ تَقْدِرُ وَلَا أَقْدِرُ وَتَعْلَمُ وَلَا أَعْلَمُ وَأَنْتَ عَلَّامُ الْغُيُوبِ اللَّهُمَّ إِنْ كُنْتَ تَعْلَمُ أَنَّ هَذَا الْأَمْرَ خَيْرٌ لِي فِي دِينِي وَمَعَاشِي وَعَاقِبَةِ أَمْرِي فَاقْدُرْهُ لِي وَيَسِّرْهُ لِي ثُمَّ بَارِكْ لِي فِيهِ وَإِنْ كُنْتَ تَعْلَمُ أَنَّ هَذَا الْأَمْرَ شَرٌّ فِي دِينِي وَمَعَاشِي وَعَاقِبَةِ أَمْرِي فَاصْرِفْهُ عَنِّي وَاصْرِفْنِي عَنْهُ وَاقْدُرْ لِيَ الْخَيْرَ حَيْثُ كَانَ ثُمَّ ارْضِنِي بِهِ

"O Allah! I ask guidance from Your knowledge, and Power from Your Might and I ask for Your great blessings. You are capable, and I am not. You know, and I do not, and You know the unseen. O Allah! If You know that this matter is good for my religion and my subsistence and in my Hereafter– (or said: If it is better for my present and later needs), then ordain it for me and make it easy for me, and then bless me in it. And if You know that this matter is harmful for me in my religion and subsistence and in the Hereafter– (or said: If it is worse for my present and later needs), then keep it away from me and let me be away from it. And ordain for me whatever is good for me, and make me satisfied with it." (Sahih al Bukhari 1166)

* When making the dua, the actual matter or decision should be mentioned instead of the words "hathal-amra" ("this matter").

MYTHS ABOUT ISTIKHARA

There are many myths surrounding istikhara. A few include:

Myth 1: Seeing a dream as the answer

Many people believe that the "answer" to istikhara comes in the form of a dream. This is one of the most common myths regarding istikhara. It's important to note that neither the Prophet (pbuh) nor the companions and first eight generations of scholars associated istikhara with dreams. There are several reasons for that. First, only prophets receive definitive messages (wahy) through dreams. For us, dreams can come from one of 3 possible sources:

1. Dreams from the nafs (*Hulm*): These are dreams that come from thoughts, experiences, emotions or desires within our self (nafs). They are not true dreams.
2. Dreams from shaytan (*Hulm*): These are dreams that come from shaytan to disturb, scare, upset or misguide us. These are not true dreams and we are told to seek refuge from Allah from these.
3. Dreams from Allah (*Ru'yaa*): These are true dreams and come from Allah.

We cannot know definitively which of these three possibilities is the source of our dreams, nor can we know definitively the meaning of our dreams. Therefore, we should not make decisions or interpret our istikhara based upon a dream.

Myth 2: Seeing a "sign" as the answer to istikhara

Many people believe that the "answer" to their istikhara will come in the form of a "sign" or a "feeling". Our hearts may or may not feel comfortable with a particular option, but our inclinations may also just be affected by what we want or believe, and not necessarily by what Allah wants or what is best for us.

<u>*Myth 3: Delegating others to pray istikhara for us*</u>

In many cultures, people ask other so-called "holy" people to pray istikhara for them. Some people even pay these people to perform istikhara for them. This was absolutely not the practice or example of the Prophet (pbuh) and the salaf. Istikhara is a prayer and duaa and should be done for oneself about any matter we need Divine direction about.

<u>*Understanding the answer and true meaning of Istikhara*</u>

If you examine the actual meaning of the istikhara duaa, you will find that it never asks for a dream or a sign or a feeling. Rather, the istikhara duaa asks Allah to *guide* and *ease* and *bless* the situation you are seeking direction on. It asks that if the situation or action is good for you, in this world and the next, then to make it happen, make it easy, and put blessing in it. And if the situation or action is *not* good for you, in this life and the next, then to take it away from you, and take you away from it, and then to bring you what is good for you and make you pleased with it.

The process of istikhara should be done alongside our research and due diligence into the matter, as well as consulting those of knowledge and expertise regarding that particular situation.

Tool 12: Tahajjud

One of the most important tools for the health and healing of the heart is the prayer in the last third of the night (tahajjud). The last third of the night is the time when Allah comes closest to us and seeks out the people who are calling upon Him.

The Prophet (pbuh) said, "Our Lord Almighty descends to the lowest heaven in the last third of every night, saying: 'Who is calling upon Me that I may answer him? Who is asking from Me that I may give him? Who is seeking My forgiveness so that I may forgive him?'" (Saḥīḥ al-Bukhārī 1145, Saḥīḥ Muslim 758)

Allah describes the people who sacrifice their sleep to call out to their Lord:

"They arise from [their] beds; they call upon their Lord in fear and hope. And they spend from what We have provided them. And no soul knows what has been hidden for them of joy, as a reward for what they used to do." (Quran 32:16-17)

تَتَجَافَى جُنُوبُهُمْ عَن الْمَضَاجِعِ يَدْعُونَ رَبَّهُمْ خَوْفًا وَطَمَعًا وَمِمَّا رَزَقْنَاهُمْ يُنفِقُونَ ۝ فَلَا تَعْلَمُ نَفْسٌ مَا أُخْفِيَ لَهُم مِّن قُرَّةِ أَعْيُنٍ جَزَاءً بِمَا كَانُوا يَعْمَلُونَ ۝

This verse is so powerful. These people forsake their beds in the depth of night to call upon their Lord. And after describing this essential spiritual habit, Allah describes the joy they will attain because of it.

FEAR AND HOPE

Allah also describes two essential qualities that these believers have: They have both fear and hope in God.

Ibn ul-Qayyim (RA), a highly respected classical scholar, wrote:

الْقَلْبُ فِي سَيْرِهِ إِلَى اللهِ عَزَّ وَجَلَّ بِمَنْزِلَةِ الطَّائِرِ فَالْمَحَبَّةُ رَأْسُهُ وَالْخَوْفُ وَالرَّجَاءُ جَنَاحَاهُ فَمَتَى سَلِمَ الرَّأْسُ وَالْجَنَاحَانِ فَالطَّائِرُ جَيِّدُ الطَّيَرَانِ وَمَتَى قُطِعَ الرَّأْسُ مَاتَ الطَّائِرُ وَمَتَى فُقِدَ الْجَنَاحَانِ فَهُوَ عُرْضَةٌ لِكُلِّ صَائِدٍ وَكَاسِرٍ

"The heart on its journey towards Allah the Exalted is like that of a bird. Love is its head, and fear and hope are its two wings. When the head is healthy, then the two wings will fly well. When the head is cut off, the bird will die. When either of two wings is damaged, the bird becomes vulnerable to every hunter and predator." (Madarij As-Salikeen)

In this profound statement, Ibn ul-Qayyim (RA) is summarizing the journey of a believer in this life. Our strongest driving force is the love of God. But we must also have hope, balanced by healthy fear and reverence for God. If the head of the bird is cut off, the bird dies immediately. If our love of God is cut off, we die spiritually. And if one of the wings of the bird is broken, the bird cannot fly straight. Similarly, if either our hope or our fear and reverence for God is weakened, we cannot be balanced in our spiritual journey. And we become more vulnerable to being misguided to going to extremes.

It is reported that the Prophet (pbuh) once entered upon a young man on his deathbed and asked him:

كَيْفَ تَجِدُكَ " . قَالَ وَاللَّهِ
يَا رَسُولَ اللَّهِ إِنِّى أَرْجُو
اللَّهَ وَإِنِّى أَخَافُ ذُنُوبِى .
فَقَالَ رَسُولُ اللَّهِ صلى الله
عليه وسلم " لاَ يَجْتَمِعَانِ
فِى قَلْبِ عَبْدٍ فِى مِثْلِ هَذَا
الْمَوْطِنِ إِلاَّ أَعْطَاهُ اللَّهُ مَا
يَرْجُو وَآمَنَهُ مِمَّا يَخَافُ

"How do you feel?" The young man replied, "By Allah, O Messenger of Allah, I have hope in Allah and I fear for my sins", The Messenger (pbuh) replied, "Never do these two feelings (of hope and fear) come together in the heart of a servant except that Allah grants the servant that which he hopes for, and saves him from that which he fears." (Jami al-Tirmidhi 983)

The Messenger of Allah (pbuh) would say the following duaa:

اللَّهُمَّ إِنِّى أَسْلَمْتُ وَجْهِى
إِلَيْكَ وَفَوَّضْتُ أَمْرِى
إِلَيْكَ وَأَلْجَأْتُ ظَهْرِى
إِلَيْكَ رَغْبَةً وَرَهْبَةً إِلَيْكَ

"Oh Allah, I submit my face to you and entrust my affair to you. I commit myself to you out of hope and fear of you." (Sahih Muslim 2710)

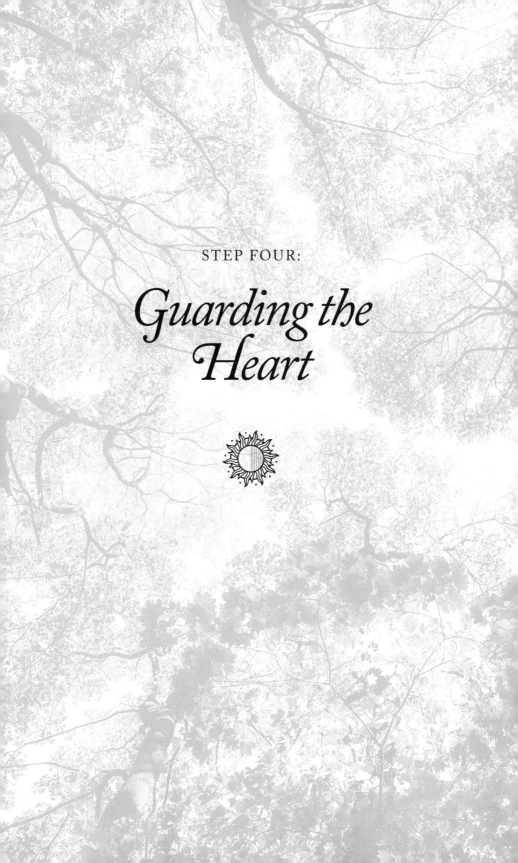

STEP FOUR:

Guarding the
Heart

Guard Your Soul Food

After we have diagnosed the root causes of our suffering, removed the barriers to healing, and treated the wound, it is essential that we guard the heart from future poisons. One of the most important ways to guard the heart and maintain healing is to guard the *openings* to the heart: *the eyes, the ears and the tongue.* People say, "You are what you eat." This is also true about "soul food". Our heart and soul will become a product of what we take in through our eyes and ears. And what we speak with our tongue. When our "soul food" is toxic, our heart pays the price. Everything we look at, or listen to, or speak, goes directly to the heart and imprints upon it. When we are constantly looking at and listening to what is haram (forbidden), we are drinking poison. Over time, our heart becomes covered with stains (*raan*).

Allah says:

"Nay! Rather, what they used to do has become like rust upon their hearts." (Quran 83:14)

كَلَّا بَلْ رَانَ عَلَى قُلُوبِهِم مَّا كَانُوا يَكْسِبُونَ ﴿١٤﴾

The other effect of what we see and hear and speak, is that it becomes our *focal point*. It grows in our heart. For example, we live in a world of appearances. All around us, we are bombarded by a hyperfocus on how things *look*. Social media, movies, magazines all worship the surface of things. When the glitter of things, the material, the appearance, is all we see, hear and talk about, it becomes more significant in our eyes. If our newsfeed on social media is only about fashion, make-up, what people are wearing, what people are eating, who is breaking up with who, this affects what is most significant in our eyes. It enlarges the importance of these things to us. Appearances, fashion, status, position, fame, dunya will become more significant in our hearts, simply because that is what we are focusing on all day. That is our "soul food".

Whereas, if we are feeding our hearts more of what really matters, more of what reminds us of Allah and our ultimate purpose, *that* will become more significant in our hearts. You are what you eat. If your "diet" is healthy, you will be healthy. Think of your daily newsfeed, what you read and watch, who and what you follow online, as the food in your fridge. That's what you will eat that day. Ask yourself, "Is it healthy or is it junk food?" Worse yet, is your fridge full of poison? Make sure that the things you're reading, the things you're looking at on your screens, the things you talk about, the things you listen to, the things that you're obsessing about, are healthy, because that's what you're eating. That's the spiritual food that you're giving your heart.

This same principle applies to fear. And this is the reason why many people end up becoming overwhelmed by negative news. When something bad happens in the world, if you obsess over all the news about that negative incident or fear, your anxiety will grow exponentially. If everything on your newsfeed or everything you're reading or watching or talking about is regarding that negative event or problem, the fear associated with the problem or event will consume and paralyze you. The darkness grows, when you focus on it. If there is darkness, light a candle. But obsessively reading, speaking, and thinking about the darkness, will not make it go away. It will only make it grow in your eyes, until you see nothing else. The other danger is that over exposure to bad/horrific news leads to desensitization to terrible news and sin.

Guard Your Company

The other crucial element of guarding your heart and maintaining healing is guarding your environment. This means keeping good company. The Prophet (pbuh) said: "A man follows the religion/way of his closest companion; so each one should consider whom he makes his friend." (Abu Dawud)

The Prophet (pbuh) also defined the best type of friend: "Your best friend is the one who, seeing him reminds you of Allah, speaking to him increases your knowledge, and his actions remind you of the hereafter." (Al-Muhasibi)

This criteria should also apply to who you marry. The one you marry is the companion who will be closest to you. And this is the person who will become an example for your children. So you must choose wisely. A woman should marry a man that she would want her son to become. And a man should marry a woman he would want his daughter to become. You should never marry someone in hopes that they will "change later". You have a responsibility to yourself and your future children to choose a good spouse and parent, to the best of your ability. So if Allah shows you who someone really is, believe Allah. If you are shown a glimpse of someone's "true colors", don't ignore it. Never turn a blind eye to what you *know*, in exchange for what you *imagine could* be. This is delusion and denial. And it has burned so many people and those around them, for the rest of their lives. Many people ignore the bad qualities and only look at appearances or "financial security" when thinking of marriage. This is a recipe for disaster. If a person doesn't pray, it is delusional to assume "they will pray later". People are on their *best behavior* in the courting phase. To presume that someone will get *better* later is very unwise. Marry a person based on who they are *now*. Never marry *"potential"*.

And remember that Allah tells us that companions who were not righteous will be enemies to each other on the Day of Judgment:

"Close friends, that Day, will be enemies to each other, except for the righteous." (Quran 43:67)

الْأَخِلَّاءُ يَوْمَئِذٍ بَعْضُهُمْ لِبَعْضٍ عَدُوٌّ إِلَّا الْمُتَّقِينَ ﴿٦٧﴾

Allah also tells us about one of the greatest regrets on the Day of Judgment:

"Oh, woe to me! I wish I had not taken that one as a friend. He has certainly led me away from the remembrance after it had come to me. And Shaitan (Satan) is ever a deserter to man in the hour of need." (Quran 25:28-29)

يَا وَيْلَتَى لَيْتَنِي لَمْ أَتَّخِذْ فُلَانًا خَلِيلًا ﴿٢٨﴾ لَقَدْ أَضَلَّنِي عَنِ الذِّكْرِ بَعْدَ إِذْ جَاءَنِي وَكَانَ الشَّيْطَانُ لِلْإِنْسَانِ خَذُولًا ﴿٢٩﴾

How a Believer Slips

Our greatest hour of need will be on the Day of Judgment. Each one of us will need to cross the bridge of *Al-Sirat*, but for some of us that bridge will be covered in darkness. Allah tells us about this scene in the Quran:

يَوْمَ يَقُولُ الْمُنَافِقُونَ وَالْمُنَافِقَاتُ لِلَّذِينَ آمَنُوا انْظُرُونَا نَقْتَبِسْ مِنْ نُورِكُمْ قِيلَ ارْجِعُوا وَرَاءَكُمْ فَالْتَمِسُوا نُورًا فَضُرِبَ بَيْنَهُمْ بِسُورٍ لَهُ بَابٌ بَاطِنُهُ فِيهِ الرَّحْمَةُ وَظَاهِرُهُ مِنْ قِبَلِهِ الْعَذَابُ ﴿١٣﴾ يُنَادُونَهُمْ أَلَمْ نَكُنْ مَعَكُمْ قَالُوا بَلَى وَلَكِنَّكُمْ فَتَنْتُمْ أَنْفُسَكُمْ وَتَرَبَّصْتُمْ وَارْتَبْتُمْ وَغَرَّتْكُمُ الْأَمَانِيُّ حَتَّى جَاءَ أَمْرُ اللَّهِ وَغَرَّكُمْ بِاللَّهِ الْغَرُورُ ﴿١٤﴾

"On the Day the hypocrite men and hypocrite women will say to those who believed, 'Wait for us that we may acquire some of your light.' It will be said, 'Go back behind you and seek light.' And a wall will be placed between them with a door, its interior containing mercy, but on the outside of it is torment. They will cry out to them: 'Were we not with you?' They shall say: 'Yes!' But you caused yourselves to fall into temptation, and you waited and doubted, and false hopes deluded you, until there came the command of Allah. And the Deceiver deceived you concerning Allah." (Quran 57:13-14)

The scariest part of this Reality is that it describes a people who began *inside* the community of believers. There was a point when they were *with* the believers. "Were we not with you?", they will ask. And the believers will confirm that these people were with them at some point. But something led them away, and they ended up on the Day of Judgment with no light. How did that happen? Allah describes the step by step process of how that happened to them.

STEP ONE: THEY PUT THEMSELVES IN FITNAH (TEMPTATION)

These are the people who placed themselves in situations where they were likely to slip or sin or become corrupted. They placed themselves in situations of fitnah. They had friends that took them away from the remembrance of God. They had company that normalized a life of sin, drinking, drugs, dating, zina (sex outside marriage), etc. And friends that only cared about this dunya. Friends that only cared about entertainment, money, power, status, fame, fashion, and having fun.

STEP TWO: THEY PROCRASTINATED IN THEIR FAITH

These people surrounded themselves with those who did not believe or practice, and so it made them put off their own practice. It made them put off faith, put off praying or wearing hijab. It made them put off purifying themselves and their lives, put off repentance and returning to Allah. And the more they put it off, the further away it slipped, until eventually their lifestyle and their procrastination began to put doubts in their own hearts about faith. Once they normalized a life of sin, they began to justify it by doubting the religion itself. And that led them to step three in the process.

STEP THREE: THEY DOUBTED

As soon as we remove the shield of remembrance of Allah from our lives, our mind starts to play tricks on us. We are no longer able to see things as they really are. Everything becomes upside down. We see what is good as being bad, and what is bad as being good. And now shaytan has open access to our mind and heart because our shield is gone.

Allah tells us:

$$وَمَن يَعْشُ عَن ذِكْرِ الرَّحْمَٰنِ نُقَيِّضْ لَهُ شَيْطَانًا فَهُوَ لَهُ قَرِينٌ ۝ وَإِنَّهُمْ لَيَصُدُّونَهُمْ عَنِ السَّبِيلِ وَيَحْسَبُونَ أَنَّهُم مُّهْتَدُونَ ۝ حَتَّىٰ إِذَا جَاءَنَا قَالَ يَا لَيْتَ بَيْنِي وَبَيْنَكَ بُعْدَ الْمَشْرِقَيْنِ فَبِئْسَ الْقَرِينُ ۝$$

"And whoever is blinded from remembrance of the Most Merciful, We appoint for him a devil, and he is to him a companion. And indeed, the devils avert them from the way [of guidance] while they think that they are [rightly] guided. Until, when he comes to Us [at Judgment], he says [to his companion], 'Oh, I wish there was between me and you the distance between the east and west - how wretched a companion.'" (Quran 43:36-38)

STEP FOUR: THEY WERE DECEIVED BY FALSE HOPES

Many people try to reduce their own dissonance and guilt by holding onto false hopes. They may hold onto the notion of God's forgiveness without taking the steps to seek it or purify themselves and their lives. They may convince themselves that what they are doing is not that bad or that others are doing far worse. For example, a woman who is struggling with guilt about not wearing hijab herself, may focus on the sins of those who do wear hijab in order to reduce her own feelings of guilt. Or a person who is living a life of sin may assume they can just "change later".

STEP FIVE: THEY WERE DECEIVED BY SHAYTAN ABOUT ALLAH

Shaytan made a vow at the beginning of time that he will seek to deceive us from every direction.

Allah tells us:

"[Satan] said, 'Because You have put me in error, I will surely sit in wait for them on Your straight path. Then I will come to them from in front of them and from behind them and on their right and on their left, and You will not find most of them grateful [to You].'" (Quran 7:16-17)

قَالَ فَبِمَا أَغْوَيْتَنِي لَأَقْعُدَنَّ لَهُمْ صِرَاطَكَ الْمُسْتَقِيمَ ۝ ثُمَّ لَآتِيَنَّهُم مِّن بَيْنِ أَيْدِيهِمْ وَمِنْ خَلْفِهِمْ وَعَنْ أَيْمَانِهِمْ وَعَن شَمَائِلِهِمْ وَلَا تَجِدُ أَكْثَرَهُمْ شَاكِرِينَ ۝

Allah allows Shaytan the freedom to attempt his deception:

"And incite [to senselessness] whoever you can among them with your voice and assault them with your horses and foot soldiers and become a partner in their wealth and their children and promise them. But Satan does not promise them anything except delusion." (Quran 17:64)

وَاسْتَفْزِزْ مَنِ اسْتَطَعْتَ مِنْهُم بِصَوْتِكَ وَأَجْلِبْ عَلَيْهِم بِخَيْلِكَ وَرَجِلِكَ وَشَارِكْهُمْ فِي الْأَمْوَالِ وَالْأَوْلَادِ وَعِدْهُمْ وَمَا يَعِدُهُمُ الشَّيْطَانُ إِلَّا غُرُورًا ۝

In the beginning, Shaytan made our father Adam (AS) slip and eat from the tree by telling him lies about Allah. And he uses the same tactic with the children of Adam. For example, before we sin, shaytan will convince us that the sin is small and Allah's forgiveness is great. Then after we sin, Shaytan will convince us to give up hope because the sin is too great and Allah's forgiveness is too small. When we go through difficulty, Shaytan will convince us that it is because Allah is angry at us or "hates us". He wants to make us stop trying. To give up hope. To hate ourselves. To drown in shame and self-loathing. Or he will deceive us through arrogance. He will use all types of deceptive tools with one objective: to get us off the straight path.

Guard Your Daily Athkar Regiment

When it comes to guarding the heart, many people believe that hardening up will protect the heart from pain. But hardening our hearts only protects us from joy. The heart was meant to stay soft. And the softer the heart, the more resilient it is. Reflect on the example given to us by the Prophet (pbuh). He compared a believer in hardship to a tender plant, versus the hardened pine. When the wind blows, the tender plant will bend and then return to its position; but the solid pine will snap.

Therefore, the way to protect the heart is to keep it soft, and to strengthen the fortress surrounding it. That fortress is built with the remembrance of God. And the heart is nourished with the oxygen and food of athkar. Every day should consist of a strict adherence to the aforementioned thikr prescription: Salah, daily athkar, and Quran. This should continue throughout the month. When a woman is on her menses, she cannot pray, but she must continue to have a regiment of thikr (athkar, duaas and Quran). Without getting into a discussion of jurisprudence, even the strictest of scholarly opinions would allow for listening to the recitation of Quran and following along with a translation during menses. And there is no scholarly opinion which limits duaa or athkar during menses.

Guard Against Corruption of the Spiritual Heart

The heart is the master of the body and it is like a sponge. It absorbs what it loves most into its core. And whatever is absorbed into the *core* of the heart *owns* the human being. There are many things that can become absorbed into the heart and cause its corruption and ruin. Imagine taking a car to the gas station and deciding to put orange juice in the tank instead of gas (petrol). What will happen to the car? Not only will the car stop running, it will break. The gas tank was created only to carry gas–not orange juice. The core of the heart was created only for God–not the creation. When we put other things, like money, career, status, or other people, into the core of our hearts, it breaks and corrupts our hearts. Even our own family, or our own children can ruin our hearts if we put them in the wrong place. Sometimes, out of His Divine mercy, Allah sends us hardships in order to remove the "orange juice from the gas tank". Sometimes the hardship will squeeze the sponge of the heart in order to remove the false "idols" of love that have become "absorbed".

Allah warns us in the Quran:

"Some people consider certain things equal to God and love them just as one should only love God. But those who believe are stronger in love for God. And if only those who have done wrong would consider [that] when they see the punishment, [they will be certain] that all power belongs to God and that God is severe in punishment." (Quran 2:165)

وَمِنَ النَّاسِ مَنْ يَتَّخِذُ مِنْ دُونِ اللَّهِ أَنْدَادًا يُحِبُّونَهُمْ كَحُبِّ اللَّهِ ۖ وَالَّذِينَ آمَنُوا أَشَدُّ حُبًّا لِلَّهِ ۗ وَلَوْ يَرَى الَّذِينَ ظَلَمُوا إِذْ يَرَوْنَ الْعَذَابَ أَنَّ الْقُوَّةَ لِلَّهِ جَمِيعًا وَأَنَّ اللَّهَ شَدِيدُ الْعَذَابِ ﴿١٦٥﴾

The word used in this ayah is *"andaad"*, which means a rival with Allah. This ayah is speaking about rivalry in *love*. When we love someone or something as we should only love Allah, that object becomes a veil between us and the Creator. And that object will also cause us deep suffering. Remember that these objects of love can come in many forms.

Stain of Absorbing Other People Into the Heart

For some hearts, the competing object of love can be another person. Allah warns us in the Quran:

قُلْ إِنْ كَانَ آبَاؤُكُمْ وَأَبْنَاؤُكُمْ وَإِخْوَانُكُمْ وَأَزْوَاجُكُمْ وَعَشِيرَتُكُمْ وَأَمْوَالٌ اقْتَرَفْتُمُوهَا وَتِجَارَةٌ تَخْشَوْنَ كَسَادَهَا وَمَسَاكِنُ تَرْضَوْنَهَا أَحَبَّ إِلَيْكُمْ مِنَ اللَّهِ وَرَسُولِهِ وَجِهَادٍ فِي سَبِيلِهِ فَتَرَبَّصُوا حَتَّى يَأْتِيَ اللَّهُ بِأَمْرِهِ ۗ وَاللَّهُ لَا يَهْدِي الْقَوْمَ الْفَاسِقِينَ ﴿٢٤﴾

"Say, 'If your fathers, your children, your brothers, your spouses, your relatives, wealth which you have obtained, business in which you fear decline, and homes with which you are pleased, are more beloved to you than Allah and His Messenger and struggling in His cause, then wait until Allah executes His command. And Allah does not guide the defiantly disobedient people.'" (Quran 9:24)

Allah lists eight different types of things we love. And every single one of those things is *halal*. Allah does not mention love for a boyfriend or girlfriend, he does not mention love of gambling or alcohol. It is all halal and even people we are supposed to love like our parents and children and relatives and spouse. So it is not loving the creation that brings upon our downfall. It is loving the creation in the *wrong way*.

For many parents–especially mothers–it can be your own child. Culturally, many mothers are even *taught* to put their child–usually a son–at the center. As a result, the mother ends up revolving her life and existence around that child. Often, even the marital relationship is put aside and only the child becomes the focus. The husband and wife become nothing more than father and mother. And the entire structure of the family becomes lopsided because the children become the foundation of that family–rather than the marriage itself. A family structure will only be strong when a strong marriage is the foundation–not the children.

Many of us are taught that once we have children, everything must be about them. We believe that self-care is "selfish" and we even stop investing in our marriage. Everything other than the child becomes secondary in our pursuit to be "good mother" and "good father". But this creates an unhealthy and unstable family structure. It also deprives the spouse of their rights when the focus is only the children. It is unjust, imbalanced and unsustainable. And it brings about a domino effect of unhealthy consequences.

For example, when a mother neglects everything else and gives her life to her son, this creates a deep rooted unhealthy attachment. When her son grows up and gets married, this mother often has great difficulty "letting go" in a healthy way. Instead, she may feel threatened by the daughter-in-law and may even set up a competitive power struggle. Many of the problems that arise between in-laws are rooted in decades-old unhealthy attachments between the mother and son. The problems are rooted in putting something other than Allah (our son) at the center and doing "*tawaf*" around it.

Not only do we harm ourselves and our marriages through this process, we also harm the child himself. Many of these children who grew up being put at the center do not develop a healthy self-concept. Instead they may become accustomed to being at the 'center' and continue to feel entitled to this treatment from their spouse and others around them. Therefore, we not only do a disservice to ourselves, our marriage and our own lives. We actually do a disservice to the child himself. We end up raising narcissists who believe the entire world should revolve around them, just as their mother did. We also raise boys who cannot easily grow into men and leaders because we handicap them by giving them little to no responsibility in the home and family. By doing everything for them, we may believe that we are giving them love; but, unfortunately, it stunts their growth and maturity and ability to grow into strong, independent, responsible *men*. Nothing should be at our center–except Allah. We should not do "tawaf" (revolve) around any created thing. And if we do, we will suffer. And those around us will suffer.

Stain of Love of Dunya

Another stain that can become absorbed into the core of the heart, causing its corruption, is the love of dunya. When we first experience this world (dunya), we become so impressed by its glitter. So we love it. Then once the glitter falls away, we become disappointed, so we hate it. Eventually we grow up further and begin to see, and interact with dunya for what it really is: Something we don't need to hate–or love. Just something we need to *use*. Allah describes dunya as a 'mata'a'. Among other meanings, '*mata'a*' is a resource, a *tool*. A tool is what you make of it. It can help you–or it can kill you. Dunya is simply the bridge you must cross to take you back *Home*. Who gets attached to a bridge? We miss the entire point by either loving or hating the bridge. The focus isn't the bridge. The focus is what's on the other side.

The Prophet (pbuh) said:

مَنْ أَشْرَبَ قَلْبَهُ حُبَّ الدُّنْيَا الْتَاطَ مِنْهَا بِثَلَاثٍ شَقَاءٍ لَا
يَنْفَدُ عَنَاهُ وَحِرْصٍ لَا يَبْلُغُ غِنَاهُ وَأَمَلٍ لَا يَبْلُغُ مُنْتَهَاهُ
فَالدُّنْيَا طَالِبَةٌ وَمَطْلُوبَةٌ فَمَنْ طَلَبَ الدُّنْيَا طَلَبَتْهُ الْآخِرَةُ
حَتَّى يَأْتِيَهُ الْمَوْتُ فَيَأْخُذَهُ وَمَنْ طَلَبَ الْآخِرَةَ طَلَبَتْهُ
الدُّنْيَا حَتَّى يَسْتَوْفِيَ مِنْهَا رِزْقَهُ

*"Whoever **absorbs** the love of this world into his heart will be entangled by three things: misery that will not leave him, greed that will never reach independence, and vain hopes that will never reach their end. For the world is seeking and is sought. Whoever seeks the world, the Hereafter will pursue him until death comes to him and it seizes him. Whoever seeks the Hereafter, the world will pursue him until he exhausts his provision from it." (Al-Mujam al-Kabir 10328, al Tabarani)*

Stain of Worshiping the Opinion of Others

Another "object" some people take and love as they should only love Allah is the opinions of others. Some people worship what others think. They make this their center and become slaves to the opinions of others. Some people live their lives obsessing over their image in front of others. Social media becomes a platform to showcase how "perfect" they are. How "perfect" their family, children, marriage, and life are. And whatever is flawed or imperfect is "photoshopped" to make it *appear* perfect. So much energy is expended in the endeavor of appearing perfect to the world, that there is no energy left to actually grow or rectify the real problems they may have. For example, some families are willing to send their daughters back to abusive husbands just so "people won't say they got divorced". This is slavery. And total oppression.

Why does this happen? Why do we become oppressed in this way and then oppress others? This oppression will happen anytime we put another thing where only God should be in our lives and hearts. We become enslaved and enslave others.

Allah tells us in the Quran:

"And [mention, O Muhammad], when Luqman said to his son while he was instructing him, 'O my son, do not associate [anything] with Allah. Indeed, association [with him] is a great injustice."' (Quran 31:13)

وَإِذْ قَالَ لُقْمَانُ لِابْنِهِ وَهُوَ
يَعِظُهُ يَا بُنَيَّ لَا تُشْرِكْ بِاللَّهِ
إِنَّ الشِّرْكَ لَظُلْمٌ عَظِيمٌ ۝

Stain of Cultural Worship

Another competitor that becomes a block on the path to God is culture. It is perfectly acceptable to partake in our individual cultures–only so long as it does not contradict a command from Allah or His messenger (pbuh). Islam did not come to eradicate cultural practices, clothing, food, etc. Islam came to direct and inform them. But when people worship their culture, they will give it precedence over the laws of God (deen). This stance is similar to the position that the Quraysh took when they refused the commands of deen because it contradicted their culture ("what our forefathers did").

The same applies with Western culture. For example, fashion will often command us to dress in a way that is in contradiction to the laws of God. The standard of beauty set by society/culture will often differ from the standard of beauty set by God (modesty). In these cases, we must decide who our True Master is. For example, Hijab is not just a cloth we wear on our heads. Hijab is an act of worship. It is a statement of the heart and limbs that we don't worship fashion or culture; we worship God. And putting on hijab doesn't mean you're perfect. And you cannot wait until you *become* "perfect" to put it on. This is a trick of Shaytan. He knows you will never be perfect, so he uses this as a barrier. Hijab is not for angels. It's for flawed, beautiful humans, saying every day that they are trying. And there is so much beauty in that struggle. God sees it. Never belittle any act of love and worship. It could be this act of obedience that God accepts, and because of it, God may forgive your other flaws.

The essence of worship is obedience. And the root of obedience is love. And so, we must ask ourselves what we *love most*; and that answer will direct us to what we *obey most*.

Is it culture? Society's standards? Fashion? Other people's perceptions and opinions?

Or is it God?

Stain of Unhealthy Attachments

Every created thing yearns to fulfill its purpose. The eyes yearn to see. The ears yearn to hear. The stomach yearns to eat. The heart yearns to love. And inside every one of us is a created thing. It is a gigantic mass. It is a mass of affection, loyalty, and devotion. And it was created with a purpose. It was created to be given. But it was made to be given in a very specific way, to a very specific place. What we choose to do—or not do—with this heavy mass, determines our state in this life and the next.

The drive to give ourselves to something compels us, and acts as a very powerful force. There is a sort of desperation to love, to share, to connect. It is a desperation to contribute, to invest, to affect. The drive is so strong; but we often don't even understand it. We often can't comprehend the nature of this inner mass, and we don't know what to do with it.

So, some of us hold on to it. To try to hold on to what was made to be given, is like holding a ticking bomb inside our chest. It finally explodes within us, creating a black hole of emptiness. This is how we implode.

And then there are some of us who do give it. But we give it in the wrong way and to the wrong hands. We try to give it, all of it—every drop of it—to our careers. We try to give it to the "love of our lives". We try to give it to this world.

To give the entirety of this mass to something other than its Creator causes unparalleled torment and inner damage.

Allah tells us in the Quran:

"Had there been within the heavens and earth gods (illah) besides God, they both would have been ruined. So exalted is Allah, Lord of the Throne, above what they describe." (Quran 21:22)

لَوْ كَانَ فِيهِمَا آلِهَةٌ إِلَّا اللَّهُ لَفَسَدَتَا فَسُبْحَانَ اللَّهِ رَبِّ الْعَرْشِ عَمَّا يَصِفُونَ ﴿٢٢﴾

In this verse, God tells us what would have happened had there been more than one object of worship in the heavens and the earth: corruption and ruin. If the heavens and the earth, in all their majesty, would have been ruined by taking more than one object of worship, what about the fragile human heart?

What happens to a heart that takes more than one object of *ultimate* love, fear, hope, and devotion? What happens to the one who gives this inner mass to something other than its Creator? What happens to the one who allows other than Allah to be soaked into the deepest recesses of the heart? Just as the heavens and the earth would have been ruined if there was another *illah* other than Allah, the heart becomes ruined when it takes another *illah*.

To understand the result of this intrusion, imagine the heart like a sponge. When something of the dunya is presented to it, the heart can either accept or reject it. If the heart is protected and rejects what is presented, the heart will remain safe. But if the heart is unprotected and accepts it, like a sponge in a container of ink, the heart will absorb. And it can absorb all the way to the core (lubb). Once this process takes place, removing that which has been absorbed becomes extremely difficult. And painful. Like cleaning out a sponge, removing what has been absorbed into the core of the heart requires agonizing and consistent squeezing.

The Prophet (pbuh) said: "Fitan (trials) will be presented to hearts, as a reed mat is interwoven: stick by stick. Any heart which **absorbs** these trials will have a black mark put in it. However, any heart that rejects them will have a white mark put in it. The result is that hearts will be of two kinds: one white like a white stone, which will not be harmed by trials as long as the heavens and earth endure; and the other dark and rusty, like an overturned vessel; not able to recognize the good, nor reject evil, but rather being absorbed with its desires." (Muslim 144)

Commenting on this hadith, Ibn ul Qayyim (RA) explains that the fitan (trials) that are presented to the heart are of two types: *shahwat* (desires) and *shubuhat* (doubt). He says, "The first causes intentions and desires to be corrupted, while the second, causes knowledge and beliefs to be corrupted." (Ighaathatul-Luhfaan, p.40)

When the fitan of desires and doubt are accepted and absorbed into the heart, there are two dangerous consequences that follow:

First, that heart will no longer be able to recognize good and evil, as they really are. If the heart is fully soaked in darkness, it may even see good as evil, and evil as good. Suddenly, the haram (forbidden) looks beautiful and the halal (permissible) looks ugly. This is the consequence of a deeply diseased heart. And that disease comes about by allowing the heart to absorb the fitan (of desires or doubt).

Second, that heart will judge and be led by whims and desires–rather than by the guidance of Allah. Instead of being a slave to Allah, such a person will become a slave to his own desires. Slavery to anything other than Allah is the most painful sort of oppression.

Even after the Children of Israel were saved from Pharoah's captivation, they were still imprisoned. They were imprisoned by the objects of worship that had entered their hearts. The object of worship was absorbed into their hearts. Allah says:

وَإِذْ أَخَذْنَا مِيثَاقَكُمْ وَرَفَعْنَا فَوْقَكُمُ الطُّورَ خُذُوا مَا آتَيْنَاكُم بِقُوَّةٍ وَاسْمَعُوا قَالُوا سَمِعْنَا وَعَصَيْنَا وَأُشْرِبُوا فِي قُلُوبِهِمُ الْعِجْلَ بِكُفْرِهِمْ قُلْ بِئْسَمَا يَأْمُرُكُم بِهِ إِيمَانُكُمْ إِن كُنتُم مُّؤْمِنِينَ ۝

"And [recall] when We took your covenant and raised over you the mount, [saying], 'Take what We have given you with determination and listen.' They said [instead], 'We hear and disobey.' And their hearts absorbed [the worship of] the calf because of their disbelief. Say, 'How wretched is that which your faith enjoins upon you, if you should be believers.'" (Quran 2:93)

Because of their misguided worship, the calf was *absorbed* into their hearts. The word used in this ayah is "*ushribu*": "to drink or absorb like a sponge". Our heart is that sponge. Today, most of us do not worship a calf, but many of us worship other forms of "that calf". We worship money, power, status and other people. And those very same objects of ultimate love, fear, hope and devotion get *absorbed* into the sponge of our hearts. As a result, our hearts become corrupted and ruined, as Allah warned in the Quran.

Allah says:

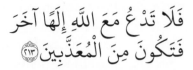

"*So do not invoke with God another deity and [thus] be among the tormented.*" (Quran 26: 213)

And that is why heartbreak is so painful. Fundamentally that excruciating pain comes from absorbing something else other than Allah into the core of our hearts. It ruins and shatters the heart itself. Taking *anything* and placing it where only God should be, in our hearts or lives, is the essence of true suffering.

And the Prophet (pbuh) has warned us of what happens when the heart becomes corrupted. He says: "Beware, in the body there is a flesh; if it is sound, the whole body is sound, and if it is corrupt, the whole body is corrupt. And behold, it is the heart." (Bukhari & Muslim)

How, then, can we prevent this corruption and ruin of the heart, and thereby the corruption and ruin of the entire body? The first way is through protection. One important Islamic principle is that protection is better than cure. For example, Allah does not tell us not to commit zina (unlawful sex), He says "Do not *come close* to zina."

The Quran says:

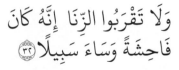

"*And do not approach unlawful sexual intercourse. Indeed, it is ever an immorality and is evil as a way.*" (Quran 17:32)

Allah does not just prohibit zina, He prohibits all that could lead to it and He puts up many barriers to even coming close: lowering the gaze, modesty in dress and behavior, avoiding seclusion with the opposite gender, etc.

In protecting the heart, Allah has also given us a prescription. The remembrance of Allah (thikr) provides layers of protection around the heart. Prayer (salah) provides a layer. Quran provides a layer. Athkar (supplications of remembrance) throughout the day provide a layer. The more we remember Allah, the more our heart is protected. *Thikr provides guards outside the heart that kill anything which threatens the tawheed or health of the heart, before it even enters.*

If, however, the heart does become infected, it must be cured. To rid the heart of what it has absorbed, you must subject it to the cleansing process. This process can be painful at first (like getting ink out of the sponge), but with consistency and patience, any heart can be remade and brought back from the dead.

Allah says,

$$أَلَمْ يَأْنِ لِلَّذِينَ آمَنُوا أَنْ تَخْشَعَ قُلُوبُهُمْ لِذِكْرِ اللَّهِ وَمَا نَزَلَ مِنَ الْحَقِّ وَلَا يَكُونُوا كَالَّذِينَ أُوتُوا الْكِتَابَ مِنْ قَبْلُ فَطَالَ عَلَيْهِمُ الْأَمَدُ فَقَسَتْ قُلُوبُهُمْ وَكَثِيرٌ مِنْهُمْ فَاسِقُونَ ﴿١٦﴾$$

"Has the time not come for those who have believed that their hearts should become humbly submissive at the remembrance of Allah and what has come down of the truth? And let them not be like those who were given the Scripture before, and a long period passed over them, so their hearts hardened; and many of them are defiantly disobedient." (Quran 57:16)

In this ayah, Allah is describing the death of a heart that happens because of neglecting the remembrance of God. But in the very next ayah, He describes the way God can give life to the dead:

"Know that Allah gives life to the earth after its lifelessness. We have made clear to you the signs; perhaps you will understand." (Quran 57:17)

This is a sign for us. Just as Allah can give life to the dead land, so too can Allah give life to the dead hearts. So if you have absorbed something of the dunya into the sponge of your heart, there is always hope.

One of the most common types of 'ink' that gets absorbed into the heart is other people. It may be a person who entered your heart, but you cannot marry. Or it may be a person you did marry, but who entered a place in the heart reserved only for Allah. Removing this person from the heart is a lot like treating a drug addiction.

If it's a person you can't be with, like a drug, you need to cut yourself off from that person completely. Cut off all communication and reminders–even if that means blocking numbers, emails, and social media profiles.

This is your detox.

Second, you need to replace that object of worship with something better. Increase in your thikr (remembrance of Allah) and get closer to Allah. If you aren't praying your daily prayers, fix that. Pray all, and pray on time. Pray tahajjud in the last third of the night (just before fajr). Make duaa (supplication), tawbah (repentance), cry, plead to Allah to cure you and heal you.

This is your treatment.

Once the treatment has taken effect, your heart will be restored, by the permission of Allah. Once the heart is restored, it can come back to balance and its created purpose: to know and love its Creator more than anything else. Such a heart will regain the ability to give again to the creation, but this time in a healthy, selfless, and less dependent way. The heart will be able to give for the sake of the One it loves most–not for the sake of the self (nafs). Once this treatment has taken effect, you will be able again to give that inner mass of complete love, devotion, and loyalty to the place it was created to live. Remember that the mass that is not given is a ticking inner bomb. But, the mass that is given to the wrong place is also a ticking inner bomb.

Give. But give rightly. Absorb. But only what rightly lives and belongs in that sacred land inside your chest. Once this balance is regained, your heart will be able to see, love, give, and take in the right way. Your heart is your true eye. Your heart is the master of the body. Its purpose is far too noble to go unrealized. Its palace is far too precious to go unguarded. Guard it. And guard it well…because every created thing yearns to fulfill its purpose.

Stain of Unguarded Words and Hurting Others

Allah says in the Quran:

"We certainly know that your heart is truly distressed by what they say. So glorify the praises of your Lord and be one of those who prostrate." (Quran 15:97-98)

First, Allah acknowledges the pain. This acknowledgement alone is healing. In fact, in counseling, one of the most important tools of therapy is acknowledging the pain and empathizing. To have someone see our pain, to not feel alone in it, to be understood. To be validated. These are extremely powerful healing forces. Now imagine it is not just another human being, but it is the Lord of the Worlds, seeing us, acknowledging us, and validating us. That alone can heal the most broken of hearts. And this is what Allah did for His Prophet (pbuh) when his heart hurt. And this is what Allah does for us. He sees us. He sees my pain. He sees your pain. He knows what is hidden in our chests. He sees our broken hearts. He knows every crack. All that we keep hidden from the world. Even what we keep hidden from ourselves.

It is also important to reflect on what caused the Prophet's (pbuh) distress described in this ayah. It wasn't the wars or physical attacks. It was words. Just words. And that is the power of words. Words can rebuild and heal–or words can destroy. And break. This is why in Islam the actions of the tongue are so heavy.

Allah's Messenger (pbuh) said,

"Whoever can guarantee [the chastity of] what is between his two jawbones and what is between his two legs [i.e. his tongue and his private parts], I guarantee Paradise for him."
(Sahih al-Bukhari 6474)

مَنْ يَضْمَنْ لِي مَا بَيْنَ لَحْيَيْهِ وَمَا بَيْنَ رِجْلَيْهِ أَضْمَنْ لَهُ الْجَنَّة

The Prophet (pbuh) said to his companions: "Do you know who is bankrupt?" They said, "The one without money or goods is bankrupt." The Prophet said, "Verily, the bankrupt of my nation are those who come on the Day of Resurrection with prayers, fasting, and charity, but also with insults, slander, consuming wealth, shedding blood, and beating others. The oppressed will each be given from his good deeds. If his good deeds run out before justice is fulfilled, then their sins will be cast upon him and he will be thrown into the Hellfire." (Sahih Muslim 2581)

Despite these fundamental teachings, many of us get religion upside down. Many people focus only on the rituals, but neglect the importance of how we treat others. And this begins with our own family. The Prophet (pbuh) said:

"The believers who show the most perfect faith are those who have the best behavior, and the best of you are those who are the best to their wives." (Jami al Tirmidhi 1162).

أَكْمَلُ الْمُؤْمِنِينَ إِيمَانًا أَحْسَنُهُمْ خُلُقًا وَخِيَارُكُمْ خِيَارُكُمْ لِنِسَائِهِمْ خُلُقًا

In this hadith, the Prophet (pbuh) has set the criterion for greatness: character and first and foremost how we treat our own families. And yet many of us have it backwards. We pray and we fast. We spend time at the masjid and wear Islamic clothing. We argue about *how* zabiha the zabiha really is. And then at the same time, we are terrible towards our families. And towards others.

Our words hold great power. Consider the way Allah describes the power of one statement that was spoken:

"When you received it with your tongues and said with your mouths that of which you had no knowledge and thought it was insignificant while it was, in the sight of Allah, tremendous." (Quran 24:15)

إِذْ تَلَقَّوْنَهُ بِأَلْسِنَتِكُمْ وَتَقُولُونَ بِأَفْوَاهِكُمْ مَّا لَيْسَ لَكُمْ بِهِ عِلْمٌ وَتَحْسَبُونَهُ هَيِّنًا وَهُوَ عِنْدَ اللَّهِ عَظِيمٌ ﴿١٥﴾

The Prophet (pbuh) once told his companions: "Restrain this!" while holding his tongue. Mu'adh bin Jabal (RA) asked: "O Prophet of Allah, will we be held accountable for what we say?" He (pbuh) said: "May your mother be bereft of you! Is there anything that topples people on their faces [or he said, on their noses] into the Hell-fire other than the harvest of their tongues?" (Related by Al-Tirmidhi, Sahih)

Our power to either build each other up or break each other down is tremendous. I knew a woman who experienced a horrific tragedy. When her son was only 6 years old, a barbecue got out of control and he caught on fire. The boy died of his injuries. I spoke to the woman and she shared her pain with me. What shocked me most was what she said caused the most lasting damage. It was the people around her. Rather than support her, she felt that the community ostracized and abandoned her. She was isolated in her grief. It was the actions and words of the people that hurt her most, as the years passed.

Allah has given us great power over one another. Great power to heal each other—or great power to destroy each other. This is the power that the angels asked about when Allah announced that He would create Adam:

"And when your Lord said to the angels, 'Indeed, I will make upon the earth a successive authority.' They said, 'Will You place upon it one who causes corruption therein and sheds blood, while we declare Your praise and sanctify You?' Allah said, 'Indeed, I know that which you do not know.'" (Quran 2:30)

وَإِذْ قَالَ رَبُّكَ لِلْمَلَائِكَةِ إِنِّي جَاعِلٌ فِي الْأَرْضِ خَلِيفَةً قَالُوا أَتَجْعَلُ فِيهَا مَنْ يُفْسِدُ فِيهَا وَيَسْفِكُ الدِّمَاءَ وَنَحْنُ نُسَبِّحُ بِحَمْدِكَ وَنُقَدِّسُ لَكَ قَالَ إِنِّي أَعْلَمُ مَا لَا تَعْلَمُونَ ٣٠

The angels already knew about the dark side of human nature. But perhaps this is why the reward is so great for those who do the exact opposite and instead bring happiness and support to others. These are the people who see others in pain or in need, and take action to alleviate that pain and fulfill that need.

The Prophet (pbuh) said:

أَحَبُّ النَّاسِ إِلَى اللهِ أَنْفَعُهُمْ لِلنَّاسِ وَأَحَبُّ الْأَعْمَالِ إِلَى اللهِ سُرُورٌ تُدْخِلُهُ عَلَى مُسْلِمٍ أَوْ تَكْشِفُ عَنْهُ كُرْبَةً أَوْ تَقْضِي عَنْهُ دِينًا أَوْ تَطْرُدُ عَنْهُ جُوعًا وَلَأَنْ أَمْشِيَ مع أَخٍ فِي حَاجَةٍ أَحَبُّ إِلَيَّ مِنْ أَنْ أَعْتَكِفَ فِي هَذَا الْمَسْجِدِ يَعْنِي مَسْجِدَ الْمَدِينَةِ شَهْرًا وَمَنْ كَفَّ غَضَبَهُ سَتَرَ اللهُ عَوْرَتَهُ وَمَنْ كَظَمَ غَيْظَهُ وَلَوْ شَاءَ أَنْ يُمْضِيَهُ أَمْضَاهُ مَلَأَ اللهُ عَزَّ وَجَلَّ قَلْبَهُ أَمْنًا يَوْمَ الْقِيَامَةِ وَمَنْ مَشَى مع أخيه فِي حَاجَةٍ حَتَّى أَثْبَتَهَا لَهُ أَثْبَتَ اللهُ عَزَّ وَجَلَّ قَدَمَهُ عَلَى الصِّرَاطِ يَوْمَ تَزِلُّ فِيهِ الْأَقْدَامُ

*"The most beloved people to Allah are those who are most beneficial to
people. The most beloved deed to Allah is to make a Muslim happy,
or to remove one of his troubles, or to forgive his debt, or to feed his
hunger. That I walk with a brother regarding a need is more beloved
to me than that I seclude myself in this mosque in Medina for a month.
Whoever swallows his anger, then Allah will conceal his faults. Whoever
suppresses his rage, even though he could fulfill his anger if he wished,
then Allah will secure his heart on the Day of Resurrection. Whoever
walks with his brother regarding a need until he secures it for him, then
Allah Almighty will make his footing firm across the bridge on the day
when the footings are shaken." (Al-Mu'jam al-Awsat 6/139, Sahih)*

The Prophet (pbuh) makes a very powerful statement in this hadith. He
says that he prefers to be in the service of another person in need than to be
in itikaf (seclusion in the masjid) for a month. And he does not indicate just
any masjid. He specifies *this* masjid–masjid Al Nabawi in Madina. This is
the masjid we spend our entire lives saving up to visit even once. The masjid
where one prayer is equivalent to 1000 prayers in another masjid.

But this hadith also teaches us another fundamental principle: when we
help others, God Himself helps us. One of the fastest routes to the assistance and victory (Nasr) of Allah is to assist others. When we are in pain,
the fastest way out of that pain is to elevate the pain of another person. This
is a Divine principle: *the way we treat others is echoed in the way God treats
us.* So we must seek the help of God by being good to His creation. In our
words and in our actions.

Healthy/Sound Heart (Qalbun Saleem)

True success is reaching Allah on the Day of Judgment with a healthy, sound
heart (qalbun saleem). This is a heart that has not been corrupted by the
absorption of false idols or competitors with God. It is a heart free from
the stain of *shirk* in any form. It is a heart that does not have "orange juice

in the gas tank". Nothing of what we chase in this life of wealth or status or power, will benefit us on that Day. All that will matter on that Day, is the condition of our heart.

Allah tells us the duaa of Ibraheem (AS) in the Quran:

"And do not disgrace me on the Day they are [all] resurrected. The Day when there will not benefit [anyone] wealth or children. But only one who comes to God with a sound heart." (Quran 26:87–89)

وَلَا تُخْزِنِي يَوْمَ يُبْعَثُونَ ۝ يَوْمَ لَا يَنْفَعُ مَالٌ وَلَا بَنُونَ ۝ إِلَّا مَنْ أَتَى اللَّهَ بِقَلْبٍ سَلِيمٍ ۝

Redefining
the Pain

The Journey to God

We are all coming back to God. It is a journey of the heart. We will shed our bodies in the grave, but we will journey on to Eternity with the same heart and soul we now carry. The body is temporary, but the heart and soul are eternal. And yet, most of our focus in this short life, is given to the needs of the temporary body, at the expense of the eternal soul.

This is tragic because every day our body is passing away. And our soul remains. The soul stays with us. If it's rotten, starved, and sick, it remains with us. Forever. We can't "shed" our soul. It follows us to our grave and then to Forever. When we leave this life, we can't come back to feed our soul. We can't come back to purify it. Our time to do that is limited. And then what we do in this temporary life for our heart and soul becomes echoed into *Eternity*. That Reality makes this life very significant. But not for the reasons many of us think it is. Not for the money or the fame or the power or status. Not for the temporary things. Not for the superficial that we chase. This life is of utmost significance because what we do in this life will have *eternal* consequences. That's big. And it should have *all* our attention.

You and I have an opportunity in this short life. We all end up with God. We all end up in a grave and then in the home of the Hereafter. And some of us will spend this life building that home, brick by brick, with our faith and our work. But, some of us will spend this life burning that house down with our own hands. We all end up at that Home. The only question is: in what condition? In what condition will our Home be? Did we build it? Or did we burn it down?

In what condition will we meet God? With a pure heart and soul? Or with a soul that has been corrupted?

Going to God in All Weather

On this journey back to God, one common spiritual myth is the idea that spirituality is what happens in "perfect", "serene", or "peaceful" conditions. We imagine a wise sage on the top of a peaceful mountain. Or a devoted worshiper sitting peacefully in a mosque. While we can most definitely find God in these fleeting circumstances, the path to God is not paved through peaceful weather. The path to God is taken in storms, sometimes running, sometimes walking, and sometimes on hands and knees. Broken. And Allah is our Healer. See, the unbroken don't need a Doctor. Allah wants us to come to Him *as we are* and from *where we are*. That's why He gives us different states and different circumstances.

Allah says:

الَّذِينَ يَذْكُرُونَ اللَّهَ قِيَامًا وَقُعُودًا وَعَلَى جُنُوبِهِمْ وَيَتَفَكَّرُونَ فِي خَلْقِ السَّمَاوَاتِ وَالْأَرْضِ رَبَّنَا مَا خَلَقْتَ هَذَا بَاطِلًا سُبْحَانَكَ فَقِنَا عَذَابَ النَّارِ ﴿١٩١﴾

"Who remember Allah while standing or sitting or [lying] on their sides and give thought to the creation of the heavens and the earth, [saying], Our Lord, You did not create this aimlessly. Exalted are You [above such a thing]; then protect us from the punishment of the Fire." (Quran 3:191)

The remembrance of God is not just something we do in good weather or in good states. It must be done in **all** conditions: standing and sitting and on our sides. When we are strong and happy, when we are weak or deprived, and when we are totally broken and lost.

Look at the lives of Allah's most beloved slaves. Prophets were given all conditions of life. Take the life of Yusuf (AS). He experienced rejection by his own family, he experienced abuse at the hands of his brothers, he experienced being enslaved, harassed, falsely accused, imprisoned, freed, and then appointed to one of the highest positions in the nation. He experienced every state. And we are to study his response in every state. At his lowest, *He turned to Allah completely.* At his highest, *He turned to Allah completely.* La illaha illah Allah. Tawheed is not a notion to be realized only in convenience. It is the very essence of the Law of the Universe. It cannot be escaped. In any direction we face, in any state we are, it is inescapable. We must witness la illah illah Allah willingly or unwillingly. Those, like our Prophets, who witnessed la illah illah Allah in every state they found themselves in were honored in the highest way. And they served as our examples until the end of time. Those, like Pharoah, who refused to witness Tawheed, still faced it, but did so debased and humiliated.

In chains.

Take the example of Muhammad (pbuh). He experienced loss from childhood. He experienced being an orphan, being poor, being rejected by his own people, being expelled from his own home, being boycotted, and losing in battle. But he also experienced victory over his enemies, power and love and loyalty. He experienced loss, pain, happiness, love, friendship, companionship, solitude, fear, strength, tears, and laughter. And we are to witness his state, his Prophetic example *in all those states*.

Take the example of our beloved Prophet (pbuh) when he was at his lowest point. When Ayesha (RA) asked him what the hardest time in his life was, he said it was the time in Taif. He was abused and thrown out— even made to bleed until his sandals stuck to his foot from the blood. And he had to walk for miles in this state of abuse against him. Yet witness his response in that state. When asked by the angels to just give the word and the mountains would crush all the people of Taif, he refused. He responded with compassion and mercy. He said that maybe there will come from them a progeny that would worship God alone. And there did.

Witness his duaa at the lowest time in his life, during the year of sadness, when he had lost his beloved wife and uncle. His duaa bears witness to his heart and his response when he was at his lowest. Tawheed. Tawheed and total reliance on Allah. He (pbuh) said: "As long as you are not displeased with me, I do not care what I face. I would, however, be much happier with Your mercy. I seek refuge in the light of Your face by which all darkness is dispelled and all matters of this life and the next are put in their right course, against incurring your wrath or being the subject of your anger. To You I submit, until I earn Your pleasure. Everything is powerless without your support."

Look at the response of the Prophet (pbuh) when he was faced with the painful accusation of disloyalty by his wife, Ayesha (AS). While most people in his situation would have been wrapped up in the assault on their pride or ego at the thought of being betrayed. Look what the Prophet's (pbuh) greatest concern was regarding his wife, who only later would be exonerated by God Himself. His greatest concern was not himself and what that possible betrayal would mean for *him*. His greatest concern was *her relationship with Allah*. He (pbuh) said: "Ayesha, I have heard this about you. If you are innocent, I expect that Allah will declare your innocence. But if you have committed the sin, you should offer repentance, and ask for Allah's forgiveness; when a servant (of Allah) confesses his guilt and repents, Allah forgives him."

Then look at his (pbuh) response when he was at his strongest. During the opening of Mecca, he did not use his position of power to take revenge on those who had harmed him and the believers. He was not proud or boastful. After securing the city, everyone gathered before the Prophet (pbuh) at the Kaaba, and he asked them tenderly, "Oh gathering of Quraysh, what do you think I will do to you?" They said, "Only good, oh noble brother, son of a noble brother." Ending the moment of suspense, he (pbuh) declared, "I will only say to you what Joseph said to his brothers, 'No blame will there be upon you today.' Go, for you are unbound." (Quran 12: 92)

We learn from the example of those nearest to Allah that we must travel the path to God in *all conditions*. *And if we are with God in all conditions, God will be with us in all conditions.*

Allah says,

"O you who have believed, if you support Allah, He will support you and plant your feet firmly." (Quran 47:7)	يَا أَيُّهَا الَّذِينَ آمَنُوا إِنْ تَنْصُرُوا اللَّهَ يَنْصُرْكُمْ وَيُثَبِّتْ أَقْدَامَكُمْ ۝

What does it mean to "support Allah" and His cause? It means to put Allah first in all conditions. To be *with* God in every condition. Seek God from *where you stand*. Seek God from where you *already are*. Don't wait to be somewhere else first. That is a deception of Shaytan. If you're feeling low, seek God *from there*. Don't wait until you "get back up". If you're afraid, seek God *from there*. Don't wait until the fear is gone. If you have sinned, seek God from where you are. Don't wait until you become "perfect" so you can be "worthy enough" to go to Him.

There is a door to Allah in every condition. If we are in despair, there is the door of hope in Him. If we have sinned, there is the door of repentance and mercy. If we are in need, there is the door of desperation and duaa. If we are lost, there is the door of seeking His guidance. If we are broken, there is the door of His Jabr. He is Al-Jabbar, the One who Mends. And if your heart has been betrayed, bound and shattered, there is the door of Al-Shafi, the One that Heals.

We must go to God when we win—and when we lose. When we're strong, and when we're weak. When we get what we want. And when we don't. When the people love and accept us, when they approve and applaud us—and when they reject and attack us. When we are rich, and when we are most needy and poor. When we are happy and content, and when we are full of sadness and despair. When we see a way out, and when it looks totally hopeless.

And we feel trapped.

Musa (AS) once looked trapped. He stood in front of the Red Sea with no way out. With only a superpower army closing in. While the people around him began to despair, Musa (AS) did not flinch.

Allah says:

$$فَأَتْبَعُوهُم مُّشْرِقِينَ ۝ فَلَمَّا تَرَاءَى الْجَمْعَانِ قَالَ أَصْحَابُ مُوسَى إِنَّا لَمُدْرَكُونَ ۝ قَالَ كَلَّا إِنَّ مَعِيَ رَبِّي سَيَهْدِينِ ۝ فَأَوْحَيْنَا إِلَى مُوسَى أَنِ اضْرِب بِّعَصَاكَ الْبَحْرَ فَانفَلَقَ فَكَانَ كُلُّ فِرْقٍ كَالطَّوْدِ الْعَظِيمِ ۝$$

"So they pursued them at sunrise. And when the two companies saw one another, the companions of Moses said, 'Indeed, we are to be overtaken!' [Moses] said, 'No! Indeed, with me is my Lord; He will guide me.' Then We inspired Moses, 'Strike with your staff the sea', and it parted, and each portion was like a great towering mountain." (Quran 26:60-63)

Allah knows that some people will only begin the journey to Him in good weather, so He gives them gifts. He knows that some people will only come towards Him in desperation, so He gives them turbulent weather. Some people come to Allah through their worship. Some crawl to Allah through their brokenness and humility. Some draw closer through their need and poverty. Some come to Allah through their mercy and forgiveness and compassion which they show to others. Some draw near to Allah through fear that pushes them to seek refuge. Some come to Allah through giving and generosity which they show to His creation. Some people even find Allah after sin, by entering from the door of repentance.

Ibn ul Qayyim writes in *Madarij as-Salikeen:*

"One of the salaf said: *'A person may commit a sin and enter Paradise because of it, or he may do an act of worship and enter Hell because of it.'*

They said: 'How is that?'

He said: 'He may commit a sin and continues to think about it, and when he stands or sits or walks he remembers his sin, so he feels ashamed and repents and seeks forgiveness and regrets it, so that will be the means of his salvation. And he may do a good deed and continue to think about it, and when he stands or sits or walks he remembers it and it fills him with self-admiration and pride, so it is the cause of his doom. So the sin may be the factor that leads him to do acts of worship and good deeds and to change his attitude so that he fears Allah and feels shy before Him and feels humiliated before Him, hanging his head in shame and weeping with regret, seeking the forgiveness of his Lord. Each of these effects is better for a person than an act of worship that makes him feel proud and show off and look down on people. Undoubtedly this sin is better before Allah and is more likely to bring salvation than one who admires himself and looks down on others, and who thinks that he is doing Allah a favor. Even if he says words that indicate something other than that, Allah is the Witness over what is in his heart. Such a person may feel hatred towards people if they do not hold him in high esteem and humiliate themselves before him. If he were to examine himself honestly, he would see that clearly.'" (Madarij as-Salikeen 1:299)

There are some people who refuse to go to Allah running, or walking, or even crawling. So they must come in chains. For some, like Pharoah, they only go to Allah through debasement and humiliation.

We all end up at Allah–willingly or unwillingly. But we can choose *how* we travel to Allah and in what state. Will we travel to Allah by choice–upright, humble, but dignified? Or will we be like Pharaoh who refused, until he was brought back to Allah, humiliated and destroyed?

Emotion and God

There's a secret about our emotions. Take fear. It either pushes us outward–to panic, withhold, and fight. Or it pushes us inward. To seek shelter, stillness, safety. And peace.

Today, when you find yourself afraid–when we all find ourselves afraid–which way are we moving? Are we angry and stressed, lashing out at those around us? Are we pushed to withhold for ourselves, or extend our hand to help others? Has our fear led us to act defensively, or rise above and act intentionally? Has it increased us in selfishness–or in compassion?

Remember, we do not live in a world of random occurrence. Everything happens with purpose and design. According to a Divine Plan. This is the tawheedi paradigm. We understand that not a leaf falls without the knowledge of the Creator. Health is a creation. And so is disease.

Emotion is also a creation. And it was created for a purpose. When you feel afraid, don't turn away from that fear.
Use it.

Use the fear itself to push you upward. Reach to find refuge in the only place that refuge really exists. Find security in Al-Mumin (The Source of Security). Find safety in Allah. If you do this, you will discover peace, even in fear. Stillness, even in the midst of chaos.
And shelter, even in the eye of the storm.

Many people do not begin the path to God because they feel unprepared or unworthy. This is one of the most deceptive tricks of the mind and shaytan. Some people think that they must first be perfect before they can try. They may think they are too broken or too sinful to try.

But Allah says in a hadith Qudsi:

أَنَا عِنْدَ ظَنِّ عَبْدِى بِى وَأَنَا مَعَهُ إِذَا ذَكَرَنِى فَإِنْ ذَكَرَنِى فِى
نَفْسِهِ ذَكَرْتُهُ فِى نَفْسِى وَإِنْ ذَكَرَنِى فِى مَلَإٍ ذَكَرْتُهُ فِى مَلَإٍ
خَيْرٍ مِنْهُمْ وَإِنْ تَقَرَّبَ إِلَىَّ بِشِبْرٍ تَقَرَّبْتُ إِلَيْهِ ذِرَاعًا وَإِنْ تَقَرَّبَ
إِلَىَّ ذِرَاعًا تَقَرَّبْتُ إِلَيْهِ بَاعًا وَإِنْ أَتَانِى يَمْشِى أَتَيْتُهُ هَرْوَلَة

"I am as My servant thinks I am. I am with him when he makes mention of Me. If he makes mention of Me to himself, I make mention of him to Myself; and if he makes mention of Me in an assembly, I make mention of him in an assembly better than it. And if he draws near to Me an arm's length, I draw near to him a cubit, and if he draws near to Me a cubit, I draw near to him a fathom. And if he comes to Me walking, I go to him at speed." (Hadith 15, 40 Hadith Qudsi)

We learn an important lesson from this hadith. First, we learn that Allah does not ask for perfection. He asks for effort. One step. The second important lesson is that even tiny effort is multiplied by God. We see this same lesson in the following hadith:

"Whosoever intended to perform a good deed, but did not do it, then Allah writes it down with Himself as a complete good deed. And if he intended to perform it and then did perform it, then Allah writes it down with Himself as from ten good deeds up to seven hundred times, up to many times multiplied. And if he intended to perform an evil deed, but did not do it, then Allah writes it down with Himself as a complete good deed. And if he intended it [the evil deed] and then performed it, then Allah writes it down as one evil deed." (Bukhari and Muslim)

Allah's mercy is not equal to His wrath. His mercy is so much greater.

Our Needs and the Attributes of Allah

Just as our emotions serve a purpose, so too does our human need. Every attribute of Allah corresponds to a human need. We need love, and Allah is Al-Wadud, the Most Loving and the Source of love. We need to feel seen and understood, and Allah is Al-Baseer, The All-Seer and Al-Aleem, the All-Knower. We need to feel safe, and Allah is Al-Mumin, The Source of Safety. We seek justice, and He is Al-Adl, The Most Just. We need provision, and Allah is Al-Razzaq, The Provider.

So Allah created the need to serve a Divine purpose. It is the *driver* that pushes us to God. And so the wise see Allah in everything. In every state. When He gives, and when He takes. In life and death. In ease and difficulty.

Whatever is from Allah is good. That means that leaving our affairs in Allah's hands is the only path to success. When we choose for ourselves, we will always be choosing from a position of weakness and blindness.

We are told in the Quran:

"And Allah wants to lighten for you [your difficulties]; and mankind was created weak." (Quran 4:28)

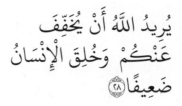

يُرِيدُ اللَّهُ أَنْ يُخَفِّفَ عَنْكُمْ وَخُلِقَ الْإِنْسَانُ ضَعِيفًا ٢٨

As human beings, we are limited in our abilities. But we are also limited in our knowledge. We have no knowledge of the unseen of any sort. This means we cannot see the future. But it also means we cannot see what is happening right now, outside of a very limited scope. Beyond that scope of hearing and seeing and perceiving or understanding, we are totally blind. Something tragic or wonderful could be happening right now in the room or building or city or country right next to us, and we would have no knowledge of it. So when we make decisions for ourselves, we make decisions blind—with little to no data. We are sightless, groping in the dark. The blind leading the blind. A blindfolded child, driving the car that is our lives. It is no wonder that we so often crash. And that families, communities, nations, so often crash. When we are Godless in our steering and in our perception, *we will always crash.*

The Quran is full of miracles. But often we only focus on the physical miracles: the splitting of the Sea, the staff turning to a snake, bringing life to the dead, and vision to the blind, by the permission of God.

But often we miss a different type of miracle. A more subtle type. We miss the miracles of the heart: The transformation of the magicians during the time of Musa (AS). The forbearance of Muhammad (pbuh) at Taif. The ability of a mother to put her own infant into the river. The forgiveness of a man for his brothers who wanted him dead.

We recognize the splitting of the sea as a sign of God. But what about the miraculous resilience Allah gave to the heart of Musa's mother? The way he "tied her heart together". What about the transformation of the hearts of the magicians? The mercy of the heart of the Prophet (pbuh) at Taif? The forgiveness in the heart of Yusuf (AS).

And Allah explains the purpose of telling us these stories in the Quran:

"And each [story] We relate to you from the news of the messengers is that by which We make firm your heart. And there has come to you, in this, the truth and an instruction and a reminder for the believers." (Quran 11:120)

وَكُلًّا نَقُصُّ عَلَيْكَ مِنْ أَنْبَاءِ الرُّسُلِ مَا نُثَبِّتُ بِهِ فُؤَادَكَ وَجَاءَكَ فِي هَذِهِ الْحَقُّ وَمَوْعِظَةٌ وَذِكْرَى لِلْمُؤْمِنِينَ ۝

Allah told these stories to the Prophet (pbuh) and to all of us, to strengthen his heart, and ours.

Dunya Formula for Success

The process of strengthening our hearts and reaching success is summarized in a powerful and comprehensive hadith:

حَدَّثَنَا أَبُو بَكْرِ بْنُ أَبِي شَيْبَةَ، وَابْنُ، نُمَيْرٍ قَالاَ حَدَّثَنَا
عَبْدُ اللَّهِ بْنُ إِدْرِيسَ، عَنْ رَبِيعَةَ بْنِ عُثْمَانَ، عَنْ مُحَمَّدِ
بْنِ يَحْيَى بْنِ حَبَّانَ، عَنِ الأَعْرَجِ، عَنْ أَبِي هُرَيْرَةَ، قَالَ قَالَ
رَسُولُ اللَّهِ صلى الله عليه وسلم " الْمُؤْمِنُ الْقَوِيُّ خَيْرٌ
وَأَحَبُّ إِلَى اللَّهِ مِنَ الْمُؤْمِنِ الضَّعِيفِ وَفِي كُلٍّ خَيْرٌ احْرِصْ
عَلَى مَا يَنْفَعُكَ وَاسْتَعِنْ بِاللَّهِ وَلاَ تَعْجِزْ وَإِنْ أَصَابَكَ شَيْءٌ
فَلاَ تَقُلْ لَوْ أَنِّي فَعَلْتُ كَانَ كَذَا وَكَذَا . وَلَكِنْ قُلْ قَدَرُ
اللَّهِ وَمَا شَاءَ فَعَلَ فَإِنَّ لَوْ تَفْتَحُ عَمَلَ الشَّيْطَانِ

"The Messenger of Allah (pbuh) said: 'The strong believer is better and
more beloved to Allah than the weak believer, although both are good.
Strive for that which will benefit you, seek the help of Allah, and do not
feel helpless. If anything befalls you, do not say, 'if only I had done such
and such', rather say: 'Qaddara Allahu wa ma sha'a fa'ala (Allah has
decreed and whatever he wills, He does).' For (saying) 'if' opens you up
to the actions of Satan." (Sahih Muslim 2664)

THE STRONG BELIEVER

In this hadith, the Prophet (pbuh) is empowering us to be strong. Faith should
not make us passive, but should rather be the very source of our strength.

STRIVE FOR WHAT IS BENEFICIAL

We must strive hard. We cannot sit passively and wait for things to happen
around us. When Hajar was stuck in the desert, she didn't just sit. She strove.

SEEK THE HELP OF ALLAH

We are totally powerless without the help of Allah. This is the essence of the statement "la hawla wa la quwat illa billah" (There is no change of state or power/might except by Allah). One of the traps many of us fall into when we are faced with hardships is that we rely on our own selves, instead of relying on Allah.

DO NOT FEEL HELPLESS

Allah tells us in the Quran: "And do not weaken, and do not despair. You will have the upper hand if you are truly believers." (Quran 3:139)

The promise of success is with the believers. Our job is only to ensure that we are *true* believers.

NO 'WHAT IFS'

One of the most painful states to be in, is the state of regret. Many people suffer greatly due to the "what ifs" that eat away at them. Here, the Prophet (pbuh) is warning us that "what ifs" open the door of shaytan. It allows him to cause us mental torment.

Allah tells us:

يَا أَيُّهَا الَّذِينَ آمَنُوا لَا تَكُونُوا كَالَّذِينَ كَفَرُوا وَقَالُوا لِإِخْوَانِهِمْ إِذَا ضَرَبُوا فِي الْأَرْضِ أَوْ كَانُوا غُزًّى لَوْ كَانُوا عِنْدَنَا مَا مَاتُوا وَمَا قُتِلُوا لِيَجْعَلَ اللَّهُ ذَلِكَ حَسْرَةً فِي قُلُوبِهِمْ وَاللَّهُ يُحْيِي وَيُمِيتُ وَاللَّهُ بِمَا تَعْمَلُونَ بَصِيرٌ ۝

"O you who have believed, do not be like those who disbelieved and said about their brothers when they traveled through the land or went out to fight, "If they had been with us, they would not have died or have been killed," so Allah makes that [misconception] an anguish within their hearts. And it is Allah who gives life and causes death, and Allah is Seeing of what you do." (Quran 3: 156)

As believers, we should have full faith that whatever has occurred was part of the decree of Allah. We learn from our mistakes, but we do not drown in them.

Transform Your Worldview

Allah says in the Quran:

*"Alif Lam Ra. These are the verses
of the Scripture, a Quran that
makes things clear." (Quran 15:1)*

الر تِلْكَ آيَاتُ الْكِتَابِ
وَقُرْآنٍ مُبِينٍ ۝

This is deep. The Quran is a source of clear guidance for mankind. But it also serves another crucial purpose. The Quran serves as a *lens* to see the world in its Reality. It is a lens that allows the Truth around us to become clear.

In other words, the Quran, in and of itself, is full of signs (ayat). But it is also a *lens* that allows us to see the signs all around us–in the heavens and the earth, and in our own lives. The Quran is a pair of glasses that allows us to see the world as it *truly* is–beyond the holograms and deception. Past the decor, flashing lights, and glitter. It allows us to see through the pain and the pleasure–the gain and the loss–to the Truth behind them. It lets us see order, behind the illusion of disorder, and meaning, behind the guise of chaos.

The Quran is the lens that shows us a deeper purpose, while others see only what's on the surface. It gives us vision of the unseen in a world that worships the material.

It is only by the lens of the Quran that one can see gifts, where others see only deprivation. Without Allah lighting our path, we get lost. When we steer for ourselves and choose for ourselves, we are sightless, groping in the dark. Allah sees everything and He is the Most Merciful. His mercy for us is greater than a mother's mercy for her own child. So with His infinite knowledge and mercy, Allah is always giving–even when it looks as though He's withholding. The wise believer will focus on what is given, rather than fixating on the illusion of what was taken.

Several years ago, my husband and I drove up to the mountains to see the autumn leaves. By the time we arrived, the sun had set. Because it was a remote area, there were almost no streetlights, so it was pitch black all around us. With the little brightness from our car headlights, all we could see was a few feet of the road in front of us. Nothing else.

The next morning, we went for a drive on the same road we had traveled the night before. We were shocked. We were surrounded by the most beautiful, massive mountains and vibrant colors everywhere. We were looking at the very same scene, but what we saw was transformed for only one reason: *there was light*. The night before, when looking at the exact landscape, all we saw was darkness. But with light, we saw the most majestic and stunning beauty. Without light, we could have an entire mountain range before our eyes, but we could not see it. This is also true in life.

Allah says:

وَالَّذِينَ كَفَرُوا أَعْمَالُهُمْ كَسَرَابٍ بِقِيعَةٍ يَحْسَبُهُ الظَّمْآنُ مَاءً حَتَّى إِذَا جَاءَهُ لَمْ يَجِدْهُ شَيْئًا وَوَجَدَ اللَّهَ عِنْدَهُ فَوَفَّاهُ حِسَابَهُ وَاللَّهُ سَرِيعُ الْحِسَابِ ۝٣٩ أَوْ كَظُلُمَاتٍ فِي بَحْرٍ لُجِّيٍّ يَغْشَاهُ مَوْجٌ مِنْ فَوْقِهِ مَوْجٌ مِنْ فَوْقِهِ سَحَابٌ ظُلُمَاتٌ بَعْضُهَا فَوْقَ بَعْضٍ إِذَا أَخْرَجَ يَدَهُ لَمْ يَكَدْ يَرَاهَا وَمَنْ لَمْ يَجْعَلِ اللَّهُ لَهُ نُورًا فَمَا لَهُ مِنْ نُورٍ ۝٤٠

"The deeds of the unbelievers are like a mirage in a desert which a thirsty man thinks is water, until he goes near and finds nothing. But he finds God before him, who gives him his due recompense. God is swift in reckoning. Or it is like the darkness of a vast, deep sea with layers of giant waves, covered by dark clouds. It is darkness upon darkness, whereby even if one stretches out his hand, he can hardly see it. One can have no light unless God gives him light." (Quran 24:39-40)

There will be many callers on our journey. We will be called in many directions, to take many paths. Our desires will call us. Our society will call us. Our culture, our loved ones, our fears, our doubts, our needs will all call to us. And without light and guidance, we can never find our way through that path, in the maze of this life. Without hope and without the courage to see light through the darkness, we will continue to stumble.

Transforming How You See Religion

There are many ways to look at religion. For some people, religion is just a sacred compartment within their lives. For others, religion is much more. *It is a sacred lens.*

The first group see religion as a compartment—a sacred room that they step into on Fridays or Sundays or during holidays. A place to practice rituals—separate from their everyday life. Those who choose this first worldview often feel scattered. For them, life is made up of many tiny pieces that they struggle to balance or keep in order. This may make them feel lost and without direction or purpose. Fragmented within their own lives.

But, there are others who see religion, not as a separate compartment of their life, but as a lens through which they view themselves, their lives, and the entire world. They are able to integrate the spiritual and the mundane into one. They are not scattered or internally fragmented. There is direction and meaning in all things. Every piece of life, the good and the bad, and the mundane, makes sense as part of a higher plan and purpose.

These are the people who can take all of their life experiences, the joy and the pain, and use it to grow and give back. These people don't feel like victims in their own lives. But rather, they become students ready to learn and grow. They are ready to fall and get back up. Stronger. They are ready to give back. They don't allow one bad outcome to deter them from their greater Purpose. They try again, even after they fail. Because they know that it was their failures, not their successes, that taught them most in life.

And because they realize that you don't drown by falling into the water. You drown by staying there.

This state can only be achieved when you change the lens with which you see the world—when you change the lens to a lens of Divine Oneness. This is tawheed. *La illaha illa Allah.* To recognize with full heart and soul that all focus, center, and purpose goes back to God. That all meaning derives from Him. That all strength and success comes from Him. And that every path that leads to Him is success–even the thorny ones. And that every road that leads away from Him is failure–even the comfortable ones.

Transforming How You See Gifts

Operate on the understanding that everything–*absolutely everything*–can be lost. Allow that realization to turn entitlement into gratitude, for each extra day, each extra minute, we have with our spouse, our children, our health, our faith, our wealth, our mental stability, and every ability, every capacity, and every faculty that we have.

Say thank you more. Smile more. Laugh. And show gratitude to God, and to the people in your life.

Every gift we have from God is just that: a gift. It's not given because we are entitled to it.

It's given because the Giver is infinitely Generous.

Transforming How You See Obstacles

When facing an obstacle, many of us focus on the obstacle's "power" to harm us. Or we focus on the harm already caused by it. What if we changed our perspective entirely? What if an obstacle became nothing more than a tool? A tool meant to refine, shape, and develop us? My teacher often says, "There would have been no Bilal without Abu Jahal." And isn't that just it? Even the existence and attempted plots of shaytan himself can end up having the opposite effect, if we are pushed more towards Allah for refuge. When we realize that the power is not with the enemy–or even the friend. When we realize that all power is with Allah alone, then every person we meet, whether friend or foe, serves a purpose. Wasn't it Musa's (AS) fear about facing Pharoah that pushed him to seek refuge in Allah? And in that seeking, was he not strengthened and elevated? And then in his final showdown with the tyrant Pharaoh, Musa (AS) was able to face the enemy head on without fear, and say with no hesitation:

"He said: By no means (shall we be overtaken)! Indeed my Lord is with me; He will guide me through." (Quran 26:62)

قَالَ كَلَّا إِنَّ مَعِيَ رَبِّي سَيَهْدِينِ ﴿٦٢﴾

It was *then* that the sea was split.

Allah's Help in Every State

There's often this quiet sadness I feel upon departures. The endings of things. The fading of autumns. The separating from loved ones. The leaving of what you know, and entering what you don't. The closings of holidays. The leavings of beautiful places and moments. That's the hard part of life. The constant movement. The change.

But why does it hurt? Because we hold onto what we know. And fear what we do not know. We find comfort and security in the familiar. But what if we didn't see it that way? What if we let go of fall, knowing that winter has its beauty too? What if we truly, truly believed that no matter how scared or unsure we are, we are never, ever alone? What if we understood that there is beauty in all seasons? That God can decorate every moment, not just the ones we know. And that He can beautify every part of the journey–not just the ones we recognize.

Ramadan

Take for example, the unprecedented experience in 2020, when Ramadan came in the midst of a global Pandemic. Many of us felt deprived. For the first time in our lives, we were unable to go to the masjid, taraweeh, qiyam. We were unable to go to family and community iftars. Many of us worried that Ramadan wouldn't be complete. And that would have indeed been the case if it were you or I who intentionally deprived *ourselves* of these things. But, not when it is the decree (qadr) of Allah. This is deep. Remember that Allah's decisions for the believer are always good for them.

The Prophet (pbuh) said:

"Amazing is the affair of the believer, for there is good for him in every matter. And this is not the case with anyone, except the believer. If something pleasing befalls him, he thanks Allah, and thus there is good for him. And if difficulty befalls him, he shows patience, and thus there is good for him." (Sahih Muslim 2999)

عَجَبًا لِأَمْرِ الْمُؤْمِنِ إِنَّ أَمْرَهُ كُلَّهُ خَيْرٌ وَلَيْسَ ذَاكَ لِأَحَدٍ إِلَّا لِلْمُؤْمِنِ إِنْ أَصَابَتْهُ سَرَّاءُ شَكَرَ فَكَانَ خَيْرًا لَهُ وَإِنْ أَصَابَتْهُ ضَرَّاءُ صَبَرَ فَكَانَ خَيْرًا لَهُ

In another hadith, the Prophet (pbuh) said:

"I am amazed by the believer. Verily, Allah does not decree anything for the believer, except what is good for him." (Musnad Ahmad 12495, Hasan)

عَجِبْتُ لِلْمُؤْمِنِ إِنَّ اللَّهَ لَا يَقْضِي لِلْمُؤْمِنِ قَضَاءً إِلَّا كَانَ خَيْرًا لَه

This means all circumstances chosen by Allah are good for us–as long as we have the response of a believer: patience and gratitude. Sometimes gifts are wrapped in deprivation and hardship. And sometimes harm is wrapped in glitter and pleasure.

Allah says, "It may be that you hate something and it is good for you, and it may be that you love something and it is bad for you. Allah knows and you do not know." (Quran 2:216)

Things are often not what they seem, but for many people, their greatest fear is that this deprivation could be a punishment or a sign of Allah's displeasure.

Now it gets even deeper. Even if the believer *has* earned the anger of Allah, deprivation can still be a gift. For the believer, it shakes them awake and inspires them to return (tawbah) and repent (istighfar). And then it inspires the believer to rectify himself. Thus, it is *still* good for them. Allah Kareem. Allah is the Most Generous. Even when He takes, He gives. Allahu akbar.

We must never think negatively of Allah. He is always giving.
The question is: Will we receive?
Will we understand with our hearts? Or will we be so stubborn to only receive the gifts of Allah when they are wrapped in the packaging *we* choose? The packaging *we* understand or are accustomed to?

Will we only accept the decree of Allah when it is what *we* want?

Like with all tests, Allah may take something away, in order to give something better—or something we need more at that time. Sometimes, Allah takes something away, so we can show sabr, and then get rewarded for our sabr. Sometimes Allah takes something away to purify us.

During Covid-19, perhaps Allah temporarily took away iftar with the community so we could reconnect with our families. Perhaps He took away our access to communal worship, so we could taste the sweetness of worship in solitude. Perhaps Allah temporarily took away access to the masjid, so we could remember that Allah is not confined to a place or time. He is always near. He is closer than our jugular vein. We can call on Him from anywhere, at any time.

And through it all, after the development and purification He wants for us, perhaps Allah could *still* reward us—as if we had still gone to the masjid. The Prophet (pbuh) said,

"If a servant falls ill or travels, the likes of what he used to do when he was settled and healthy will be recorded for him." (Sahih al-Bukhārī 2996)

إِذَا مَرِضَ الْعَبْدُ أَوْ سَافَرَ كُتِبَ لَهُ مِثْلُ مَا كَانَ يَعْمَلُ مُقِيمًا صَحِيحًا

Remember the lesson which the Prophet (pbuh) instructed our mother, Umm Salamah (RA): That even through deprivation, we can be given. He (pbuh) said, "There is no Muslim who is stricken with a calamity and says what

Allah has enjoined – 'Verily to Allah we belong and unto Him is our return. Oh Allah, reward me for my affliction and compensate me with something better' – but Allah will compensate him with something better." (Muslim 918)

Only when we change our lens, will what we see around us begin to change. We choose. We can continue to see only what is lost, and all that we miss. Or, we can look deeper.

Ibn ul Qayyim writes: "From the perfection of Allah's ihsan is that He allows His slave to taste the bitterness of the break before the sweetness of the mend. So He does not break His believing slave, except to mend him. And He does not withhold from him, except to give him. And He does not test him (with hardship), except to cure him."

Remember Allah never deprives the believer. He is always giving to the believer. This must become a solid foundation of our understanding of Allah. We must hold this knowledge firm in our hearts. So if a circumstance is by the will and decision of Allah, it must be good for us—even if it's a gift wrapped in something we dislike.

Often it is the most bitter medicine that ends up becoming our cure.

And so, we should never fear the storm itself. We never *ask* for storms. But, if a storm hits our life, we should find security in knowing that Allah will carry us through. He gives us the capacity and the help to bear it. He heals us and mends our hearts to become even more beautiful than before it broke. He gives us ease (yusr) and blessings along the way (collateral beauty). He purifies and strengthens us through it (post traumatic growth). And then after it all, He gives us an unending reward (the reward of sabr is without measure).

Sometimes Allah carries us through our pain in the most miraculous ways. Ramadan is one of those miraculous ways. It comes again and again to save us from ourselves. Some of us have fallen into despair, wondering when the help of Allah will come. Some of us are drowning in sin. Some of us are ready to give up. For many of us, the night has been long and it may feel as though the night will never end.

But Allah's help is promised, and no darkness lasts forever. Allah sends Ramadan like a rising sun at the end of a long night. He sends this month of mercy and hope to save us from ourselves. To liberate the souls shackled by despair and free the hearts enslaved to sin. To show us that truly with hardship, comes ease. And to remind us that no night lasts forever because the decree of Allah is swift and inescapable. And so we bow. We bow to

His power. We bow to His mercy. We bow to the opportunity to show our gratitude for this gift.

Let each Ramadan be a time of renewal. Transformation. And change. A chance to change our lives and ourselves. An open stage to demonstrate to our Lord that, indeed, we hear and we obey. That indeed we love our food and our water. But we love Him more.

Let Ramadan be an opportunity to show our gratitude for another year of life. Of health. Of faith. Another year to witness this month, while so many others could not. And let it be a month of service and compassion towards ourselves and others. Let our kindness begin with our families and extend to others. For truly the best of you are best to their family.

And finally, let it be a time to let go of the chains that have bound us to the past–to the pain, the mistakes, the regret. Let us free ourselves from the grudges and the rage. Let us finally let go and let God. Let us mend what was broken and begin again. Let us see this new moon as a new start. For all of us. A new chance to let go. To heal.
And then rise again.

Transforming Our Life Experiences

In order to rise through our pain, we must change the way we see it. *As we go through life, we often become so fixated on trying to understand **why** things happen, that we become distracted from **how** we should respond.* There is an amazing way to transform every life experience into a blessing. That power is ours. And that power lies entirely in how we respond. We are taught in the Quran and sunnah that every life experience is given to us for one or more of these three reasons: as a punishment, a blessing, or a test.
If we examine each of these possibilities and respond appropriately, every experience–the easy and the hard–can become a blessing.

PUNISHMENT

Rather than wasting our mental and emotional energy asking *why,* and wondering if we are being punished, why not focus instead on our response. If we repent, then every experience–even one that could have been a punishment–becomes a blessing. And a means of purification.

BLESSING

The way to transform any provision given to us by God into a blessing is to show gratitude for it. Showing gratitude (*shukr*) also increases our blessings, as taught by the Divine Quranic formula.

Allah said:

"And [remember] when your Lord proclaimed, 'If you are grateful, I will surely increase you [in favor]; but if you deny, indeed, My punishment is severe.'" (Quran 14:7)

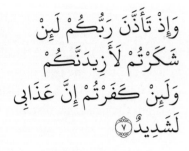

TESTS

There are times when our life experiences are tests for us. Allah places people and life events on our path to create the opportunity for us to be patient, to serve, to repair, to shine. To demonstrate sabr. Every life experience is an opportunity. Rather than getting caught up in *diagnosing* every aspect of our life, we can focus our energy on *using* every aspect of our life to become better.

Without trying to "play God" and understand the inner workings of His Divine plan, we can transform every hurdle into a steppingstone. By consistently living a *lifestyle* of repentance, gratitude, and patience, we can turn every obstacle into a tool. And live a life of spiritual and psychological flourishing.

Prophetic Formula for Healing

When we study the examples of the Prophets, we find a divinely inspired blueprint for healing. They all provided the epitome of what a believer should be in hardship. Take the example of Ayoub (AS) in the deepest part of his pain after losing his children, his wealth, and his health:

"And Job (Ayoub), when he called to his Lord, 'Indeed, adversity has touched me, and you are the Most Merciful of the merciful.'"
(Quran 21:83)

وَأَيُّوبَ إِذْ نَادَى رَبَّهُ أَنِّى مَسَّنِيَ الضُّرُّ وَأَنْتَ أَرْحَمُ الرَّاحِمِينَ ﴿٨٣﴾

Despite Ayoub's (AS) pain, he continues to have full hope in Allah. When we examine the example of Yaqoob (AS), we discover the very same lesson. He had lost two of his sons and his eyesight by this point. In the midst of his pain, He called out to Allah:

قَالَ إِنَّمَا أَشْكُو بَثِّي وَحُزْنِي إِلَى اللَّهِ وَأَعْلَمُ مِنَ اللَّهِ مَا لَا
تَعْلَمُونَ ﴿٨٦﴾ يَا بَنِيَّ اذْهَبُوا فَتَحَسَّسُوا مِنْ يُوسُفَ وَأَخِيهِ
وَلَا تَيْأَسُوا مِنْ رَوْحِ اللَّهِ إِنَّهُ لَا يَيْأَسُ مِنْ رَوْحِ اللَّهِ إِلَّا
الْقَوْمُ الْكَافِرُونَ ﴿٨٧﴾

"He said, 'I only complain of my suffering and my grief to Allah, and I know from Allah that which you do not know. Oh my sons, go and find out about Joseph and his brother and despair not of relief from Allah. Indeed, no one despairs of relief from Allah except the disbelieving people.'" (Quran 12:86-87)

Within these examples, we can extract a powerful formula for healing, in the midst of deep pain and loss:

Turn to Allah Alone

First, you will see that each and every one of them turned wholeheartedly to Allah alone. Allah was their ultimate Source of help and comfort and healing. He was the ultimate Focus. This is essential. If we turn to other than Allah with our whole heart, we will only suffer more. And we will continue to suffer until we stop and turn around. And return (*Tawbah*). *Ikhlas* is to seek Allah purely without the stain of the creation. *Sidq* (truthfulness) is to seek Allah purely without the stain of *Nafs* (self).

Be Honest Without Armor

There can be no healing without being honest with yourself and God. How can we heal a wound, if we've covered it up and pretend it isn't there?

Imagine going to a doctor after a gunshot wound and pretending that we only have a papercut.

We must be able to remove our armor and masks and be real with ourselves and God. Ayoub (AS) did not pretend. He was honest about his pain. He called out: "Affliction has touched me." Yaqoob (AS) likewise was honest about his pain. He cried out: "I only complain of my suffering and grief to Allah." He admits his grief to himself and God.

Have Hope

We know that those closest to Allah were tested in their lives, in their families, in their health. Their trials were severe. Their pain was deep. Every Prophet experienced great hardships. And yet every single one of them never lost hope in Allah and His mercy. This was their focal point. This was the Divine rope they never let go of, despite the circumstances. Their storms, though severe, never drowned them because they held onto the rope of Divine hope.

Even in the very depth of his anguish, Ayoub (AS) was focused on the mercy of Allah. He said, "And You are the Most Merciful of the merciful." Yaqoob's (AS) grief had gotten so deep that he cried until he lost his eyesight. And now he had lost his second son as well. And yet, in the very midst of *that* grief, Yaqoob (AS) did not lose hope in Allah. He told his sons, "Oh my sons, go and find out about Joseph and his brother and despair not of relief from Allah. Indeed, no one despairs of relief from Allah except the disbelieving people." This is a man who had gone blind from grief. A man whose son was taken away from him and now his second son was gone. Yusuf (AS) had been lost for 40 years, and yet Yaqoob (AS) continued to have hope in reuniting with him.

Take Action

Yaqoob (AS) did not despair. He turned to Allah completely. He was honest and real with himself and Allah. But he also *took action* and instructed his sons to take action to remove his suffering. He said, "Oh my sons, go and find out about Joseph and his brother."

Expanding Your Chest and Holding Your Heart Together

When Musa (AS) was facing the greatest challenge of his life, he asked Allah to "expand his chest". This didn't remove the difficulty; he still had to face Pharoah. But his task became smaller in comparison to the expansion and help of Allah. When the mother of Musa (AS) had to face the greatest challenge of her life, Allah held her heart together (*rabatna ala qalbiha*). She still had to put her child in the river, but Allah held her together, *through* that trial. And then He returned her child to her.

When you face the greatest challenges of your life, ask Allah to expand your chest and hold your heart together. If Allah does this, the mountain may not move, but He will allow you to climb it. The fire will not disappear, but Allah can command it to be *cool and a place of safety*, as He did for Ibrahim (AS). He will carry you through. The mountain shrinks and your capacity increases. The fire cools, and your inner peace deepens.

This is the help of Allah. Allah does not promise the believer that there will be no storms in this life. These storms will always come. But Allah promises the believer that He will carry them through their storms, if they turn to Him.

And remember that the heart is a tank. If you don't let the tears out, the tank explodes. Remember that you've been here before. Remember that. And Allah has always, always saved you.

There is peace after the rain. Even the sky finds relief through tears. But you cannot rely on yourself. You cannot carry this mountain on your own. It will crush you if you do. You must hand the mountain to Allah. No challenge is a burden to the Creator of the heavens and the earth.

The challenge itself is a creation.

Finding Our Way Home

We began with God. And we will return to God. We left our home in paradise and began a spiritual journey through this life. Our ultimate goal is to find our way back home with God and to return with a sound heart.

But as we journey through this life, we will face every kind of storm. And each and every one of those storms has the potential to either destroy us or to shape us into the person we are meant to be. In one of my favorite X-Men quotes, as Wolverine is being crafted, he is told: "We're gonna make you indestructible. But first, we're gonna have to destroy you."

There is something to be said about the resilience and the growth that can only be had through our challenges. Cynthia Occelli wrote: "For a seed to achieve its greatest expression, it must come completely undone. The shell cracks, its insides come out, and everything changes. To someone who doesn't understand growth, it would look like complete destruction."

We all wish our paths could be easy and painless, but we often forget a fundamental principle. If you ask a personal trainer to make you strong, she won't have you sit on the couch. She won't make you "comfortable". That trainer will add more weight and more difficulty. We understand this principle in the physical world; we understand that it is actually through *discomfort* that we grow. Strength comes from lifting and endurance is born from challenge. In the physical world, the process itself is called "resistance training".

And so here we are in the midst of our journey back Home. God is our Trainer and life is our gym. Theodore Roosevelt once said: "It is not the critic who counts; not the man who points out how the strong man stumbles, or where the doer of deeds could have done them better. The credit belongs to the man who is actually in the arena, whose face is marred by dust and sweat and blood; who strives valiantly; who errs, who comes short again and again... who at the best, knows in the end the triumph of high achievement, and who at the worst, if he fails, at least fails while daring greatly."

That's who we must be. The men and women in the arena. Those who did not always have it easy and so we learned how to keep going, even when the world around us shut down. Because even if you can't move, you can pray. Tell God you're still trying. It will get easier. You're being trained. Believe me the training hurts sometimes. And we are always being trained. In ease, and in hardship. And what could be more beautiful than the mercy of a Trainer who doesn't expect perfection?

To seek perfection in the hilltops of our life is to completely miss the purpose of the journey. That purpose is to strive, slip, bleed, bruise, break sometimes. And then to get back up. And then to run, or walk, or crawl. But to get back up. Not because you are strong, but because *He is*. Because *your Goal is*. If what you seek is beautiful, you become beautiful. If what you seek is strong, you become strong. **But if you seek perfection in either yourself or in the journey, you will lose hope with each empty hilltop.**

The journey isn't perfect and neither is the traveler. But that's the Design. That's as it should be. It was designed to make the traveler keep going. Keep seeking. Keep trying and hoping. God tells us all to come. Those on the hilltop, and those in the valley. Those with broken bones and those with skinned knees; *God wants us all.* Despite our brokenness, the traveler must never stop. Because while the journey and the traveler aren't perfect, the destination *is.* And *that* is what should keep you going, even when all you want to do is give up.

Hajar did not run once. She did not see "results" at the beginning. She ran between Safa and Marwa *seven times*. She only saw "results" after the *seventh* time. But what about the first six times? Were they useless efforts?

Why are we asked to go between Safa and Marwa as part of one of the greatest acts of worship in our deen (sa'ee)? Will our sa'ee–which literally means "striving"–bring water from the sand? Why are all Muslims asked to do this action that will not bring any "result" (zamzam from the sand)?

By making the *process* the goal, Allah teaches us that the *process itself* is the worship. *Not the result.* There is an immense reward for hajj and umrah. And no hajj or umrah is valid without Sa'ee. So by emulating Hajar's **process**–not her result–we are rewarded immensely.

In our lives, we will often have to "do sa'ee": actions we take, struggles we fight, repeated efforts we do. And sometimes we won't see immediate "results" or outcomes. Often we might feel that the effort itself was useless. But the story of Hajar (AS) and the resulting religious obligation teaches us a profound lesson. The process itself is the worship. And even the results that we do see, require a process.

Even our so-called "failures" become part of our success. Thomas Edison failed one thousand times before he finally invented the light bulb. Albert Einstein didn't speak until he was four and his teachers thought he wouldn't amount to anything. Bill Gates failed in his first business, and Walt Disney was fired for not being creative enough. Steven Spielberg was rejected twice by a film school, and Stephen King had his most popular book rejected thirty times before it was published. He actually threw away the manuscript in the trash out of despair. Today, he has over fifty novels selling more than 350 million copies.

But this phenomenon is not isolated. In 1962, a psychologist by the name of Victor Goertzel and his wife published a book called *Cradles of Eminence: A Provocative Study of the Childhoods of over 400 Famous 20th Century Men and Women*. He selected famous individuals who had made significant contributions to society. What he found was striking. *A full 75 percent of them came from a background full of misfortune, such as neglect, poverty, abuse, or illness.* "The normal man," Goertzel writes, "is not a likely candidate for the Hall of Fame."

In another fascinating study of more than two thousand people, aged 18-101, individuals who had experienced some adversity were both higher functioning and more satisfied with their lives.

D.H. Lawrence writes: "Ours is essentially a tragic age, so we refuse to take it tragically. The cataclysm has happened, we are among the ruins, we start to build up new little habitats, to have new little hopes. It is rather hard work: there is now no smooth road into the future: but we go round, or scramble over the obstacles. We've got to live, no matter how many skies have fallen."

On this journey back to God, you will witness many skies falling. But never, ever think it is the End. When the skies start falling, you will think that you have to stand tall against the storm. That you have to figure it out on your own. That you have to be "strong" and fix it yourself. And then you will reach a breaking point. And when you do, you will have to make a decision that will determine your success. Or your failure. Every cell in your body will scream to give up. To put down your sword and stop fighting. Everything will tell you that there's no use, and that it will never work. That things will never change. That's how you'll know you've gotten there. And that's how you'll know what you have to do next.

Listen carefully.

This is where you will have to bow. But don't break. This is what will distinguish the ones who keep going, and the ones who drown. The ones who drown will be those who refuse to bend and refused to kneel. You will need to bend when you get there. You will need to kneel. Submit and find your strength in humility. Stop trying to be "strong". Stop trying to steer. Hand over the reins only to God. And stay there in prostration. Not only with your body. With your entire heart. Stay in prostration with your life. Submit. Prostrate. Recognize your humanity. Your need. Your dependence. And recognize His power. Recognize that He is Lord and you are His creation. Recognize that He created you *in order to save you*. He created the storm in order to save you from it.

This is profound.

Dear beautifully flawed human, seek power in your humanness. And therefore in your need for the One with no need or flaw. Seek power in His power and therefore your capacity to be both human and beautiful, both flawed and inspired. The Divine design is always perfect. *Always*. You can't break or improve on that design. Dear human, you are flawed because you were designed that way. You were designed that way so that you would find the strength and beauty in relying entirely on the Flawless.

To seek perfection within yourself is to miss the point entirely. Everything in you was designed to make you seek Him. To push you back to Him. Everything in this life was designed to make you seek the Home with Him. If you were 'perfect', you wouldn't be pushed to seek His perfection. And if this life were perfect, you wouldn't seek the perfection of the next.

This life, our entire journey here, is not an end. It is a purposeful process, designed by God to shape our hearts. To prepare our souls for the Final Meeting with Him. Allow the process to refine you. Allow it to remake you. It will hurt. It will seem like the end so many times. But it is not the end. Your journey will keep going and you will rise out of your pain, stronger.

And in the End, it won't be how you walked in the sun—but how you handled the storm—that will determine your victory. It won't be about how you ran. It will be about how you fell, and then got back up. It won't be about how you shined in the light. It will be about how you managed the darkness, inside and outside yourself.

I don't cringe at the old pictures anymore. The emptiness in my eyes. The pain I walked with. Those are my battle wounds. They prove I've been there. I've lived. I've suffered, yes. But, it didn't kill me. I survived. I got back up and I kept going. Every time. I got back up.

Because in the end, it won't be about your triumphs, or mine. It will be about how you took defeat. It won't be about how you performed when you were strong, but how you did while bound and broken. It won't be about your ability to walk. It will be about your willingness to crawl—even when you're hopeless. It won't be about what you did when you won. But who you were after you lost. Again.

Because character isn't made on the shore. Character is born in the waves. The crushing kind.

The kind of waves that tell you to give up because there is no point in trying again.

The kind of waves that tell you that the ocean is too mighty for you, and you don't stand a chance.

You see, heroes aren't known by their trophies. They're known by their scars.